BATH HISTORY

BATH HISTORY

VOLUME XI

edited by Graham Davis

Bath Preservation Trust
2009

Bath History Committee: Michael Rowe (Chairman), Edward Bayntun Coward, Stephen Bird, Daniel Brown and Graham Davis. All their hard work is gratefully acknowledged.

First published in 2009 by Bath Preservation Trust, No 1 Royal Crescent, Bath

Typeset in Palatino

Printed in Great Britain by B A S Printers, Romsey, Hants

ISBN 978-1-898954-05-7

British Library Cataloguing-in-Publication Data:
a catalogue record for this book is available from the British Library

Contents

Editorial

Bath History is back. After the milestone of ten volumes published over twenty years, there is an opportunity for some fresh thinking in the preparation of future volumes. So there is a new and larger format, with a greater emphasis on visual images in support of the written texts, new features, and a new team of specialist advisers, supporting a new committee and editor. Some changes then from past editions but also a continuity that seeks to maintain the quality of research and writing that was the hallmark of the first ten volumes. In working on the material for this volume, I have been increasingly aware of the heroic achievement of the previous editors, Simon Hunt, Trevor Fawcett and Brenda Buchanan. Editors like historians always follow in the footsteps of predecessors.

In addition to well-established scholars, Bath History includes articles from research students and unpublished writers who have material that breaks new ground in our understanding of the city's rich history. New and exciting writing is a feature of volume XI as part of a broad brief in terms of what constitutes Bath history. People who have contributed to the city (some of whom were outsiders), as well as places of interest within it, are represented in a history that incorporates archaeology, medical history, social history, business history, social policy and the arts.

From the list of contents, readers will see some new features, such as the interview with a Bath historian, a piece on plans on the Royal Crescent that were never implemented, as shown in the Exhibition held at the Victoria Art Gallery, and an ephemera piece on Charles Dickens and a Guild of Literature and Art ticket of 1851.

With the current Southgate development, it is appropriate to feature the historical investigation of early maps and other documents by Elizabeth Holland, Mike Chapman and Colin Johnston that provides the material for the story of the horse baths in the Southgate area of the city. Jan Chivers' article on James and George Norman and the rise of the Casualty Hospital (the foreunner of the modern R.U.H.) is a fascinating story of charity and social advancement. Jackie Collier's piece on the Irish philanthropist, Lady Isobella King, is a reminder that glass ceilings are there to be broken. She was able to achieve a great deal through her charity work in Bath in a patriarchal society that excluded women from public life. A neglected source for the social history of crime, stunning photographs of criminals held by the Bath Police, illuminates the piece on Crime and Criminal Portraits in Victorian and Edwardian Bath. Graham Davis argues that Victorian notions of crime were determined by ideas of social class, and in Bath, the pattern of criminal activity reflected the city's unusual social structure.

With migration another topic of current interest, it is timely to feature Stuart Burroughs' piece on the life and career of Gustav Horstmann, the German clock and watchmaker, whose company became a household name in the city. Malcolm Hitchcock's close study of early municipal housing in Bath is lavishly illustrated, and recalls how pioneering social policy affected the lives of thousands of Bath citizens in the twentieth century. Tim Bullamore has written an outstanding piece on Yehudi Menuhin and Bath, showing how Menuhin's career and the Bath Festival gained from his association with the city. It is a deeply moving account of Menuhin's life and his importance to the cultural life of modern Bath. Dan Brown's research for the brilliant photographs that illustrate the piece and adorn the cover should be also be acknowledged, as well as his rapidly growing photographic archive of Bath in Time, extensively drawn on for the production of this volume.

For our first interview, we have two distinguished Bath historians, Dr. John Wroughton in conversation with Elizabeth Holland. What is revealed is a fascinating life history as well as a life devoted to the history of Old Bath.

At the start of the planning for this volume a group of specialist advisers were assembled: Daniel Brown, Stuart Burroughs, Peter Davenport, Michael Forsyth, Amy Frost, Elizabeth Holland, Colin Johnston, Gillian Sladen, Susan Sloman, Cathryn Spence and John Wroughton. Their collective wisdom and expertise has been drawn on and will contribute increasingly to future volumes. Bath is fortunate in having such a range of specialist knowledge to call on.

All of us connected with Bath History hope you will enjoy the new look and contents of volume XI. Your comments will be welcomed. Please send them to: editor@bathhistory.org.uk

Graham Davis,
editor.

No 1 Royal Crescent c.1978 by Peter Coard.
Bath in Time – Private Collection

No 1 Royal Crescent, the home of the Bath Preservation Trust, whose generous support has made this publication possible.

Notes on Contributors

Anne Buchanan – Having never previously visited the city, Anne came to Bath nearly six years ago to catalogue the local history book collections. Over 10,000 items and three years later, Anne transferred to the post of Local Studies Librarian at Bath Central Library. She remains enthusiastic about historical research and the variety of enquiries and range of items in the collections. Before Bath, Anne worked in the Caird Library of the National Maritime Museum at Greenwich. At St. Andrews University, she gained an MA in Scottish History and an M.Phil. in Maritime History.

Stuart Burroughs – is a Bathonian and has been Director of the Museum of Bath at Work since 1992. He is presently Chairman of the Bath & North East Somerset Museums Group, is a trustee at the Bath Royal Literary and Scientific Institute and recently retired as Chairman of Bristol Industrial Archaeological Society. He has lectured widely on the social and commercial development of Bath and its surroundings and in addition to having articles published on the subject was, in 2003, co-author of *Stothert & Pitt: The World's Cranemakers* with Ken Andrews.

Mike Chapman - trained as a cartographic surveyor and gained archaeological experience with William Wedlake. He works as an historic landscape consultant for BANES, previously with Avon, and edits the journal of the Bristol Industrial and Archaeological Society. He is chair of the Survey of Old Bath and joint editor of the Society's magazine.

Jan Chivers - After a career in Primary Education, Jan obtained a Combined Honours BA from Bath Spa University, followed by an MA in Local and Regional History. She graduated from the University of the West of England with a PhD in July 2007. Her doctoral thesis was based on Poor Law records, charity records and Coroners' records for the city of Bath for the period 1775 to 1835. Her publications include 'Bath Penitentiary and Lock Hospital, 1816-1824' in *Women's History Magazine*, Issue 51, Autumn 2005, and 'Infanticide in Bath, 1776-1835' in *Bath Exposed! Essays on the Social History of Bath, 1775-1945*, edited by Graham Davis,(2007). Jan is currently researching the life and work of John

Curry, overseer for the parish of Walcot in the early nineteenth century and writing an historical novel set in late eighteenth-century Bath.

Jackie Collier - is a PhD student at Bath Spa University. After completing an MA in Bath History and Culture in 2006, specialising in gender and philanthropy at the beginning of the nineteenth century, she was awarded a scholarship by the Arts and Humanities Research Council to research more specifically the role of elite women in philanthropy in early nineteenth-century England.

Graham Davis - retired this year as Professor of History at Bath Spa University after nearly forty years service. His publications on Bath's history include *Memoirs of a Street Urchin* (1985), *Bath Beyond the Guide Book* (1988), co-author with Penny Bonsall, *Bath: A New History* (1996), and *A History of Bath: Image and Reality* (2006), editor of *Bath Exposed!: Essays on the History of Bath, 1775-1945* (2007), and author of the forthcoming, *Competing Images of Victorian Bath: The City and the Slum* (2009). He has also written extensively on Irish migration: *The Irish in Britain, 1815-1914* (1991) and the award winning *Land!: Irish Pioneers in Mexican and Revolutionary Texas* (2002).

Malcolm Hitchcock - spent his working life as an aeronautical engineer in Bristol, the last ten years managing a Design Department. On retirement, he completed a study of the history of Bath's municipal allotments, and from this an examination of public housing was a natural progression, since they often stood side-by-side to provide for the less well-off members of society.

Elizabeth Holland - graduated in history and economics and has lectured on both subjects. She is the founder and secretary of the Survey of Old Bath, which aims to research and reconstruct the city and the lives of its citizens. She is joint editor of the Survey's magazine, *The Survey of Bath and District*, and has written many articles on old Bath, including with Mike Chapman, 'The Development of the Saw Close from the Middle Ages' in *Bath History, Vol. VIII* (2000).

Colin Johnston - is the Principal Archivist of Bath Record Office and the city's first professional archivist. Colin has spent the past twenty five years in the basement of the Guildhall sorting out the Record Office archive collections and ensuring all who ask can have access to the records. His long service record bears witness to his patience in working towards his ultimate goal of seeing archives and researchers housed in premises befitting Bath's World Heritage City status.

Katharine Wall - is Collections Manager at the Victoria Art Gallery in Bath, and has curated local history exhibitions including: 'Bath As It Might Have Been', 'Life in Georgian Bath', and 'Stewing Alive: The Story of Bathing in Bath'.

Dr. John Wroughton - read Modern History at Oxford and was formerly Headmaster of King Edward's School in Bath. After 'retirement' in 1993, he lectured part-time at the universities of Bath and Bristol for their adult education programmes. A Fellow of the Royal Historical Society, he now lectures extensively on seventeenth-century topics throughout the West Country. His many publications include *A Community at War: the Civil War in Bath and North Somerset* (1992*); The Stuart Age, 1603-1714* (1997); *An Unhappy Civil War: the Experiences of Ordinary People in the Western Counties, 1642-1646* (1999); *Stuart Bath: Life in the Forgotten City, 1603-1714* (2004); *Tudor Bath: Life and Strife in the Little City, 1485-1603* (2006); and *The Battle of Lansdown, 1643: An Explorer's Guide* (2008). A contributor of nine biographies to the *Oxford Dictionary of National Biography* (2004), he was also General Editor of the 26–volume series, *Documents and Debates* published by Macmillan.

Bath Spa for Horses – Two Thermal Horse Baths and their sites

Elizabeth Holland, Mike Chapman and Colin Johnston

BATH'S TUDOR HORSE BATH has been made famous by the map inset with Speed's map of Somerset, first published in 1610. The bath is shown lying in the present Southgate redevelopment area, to the east of the Tudor Southgate Street. The map shows a horse sporting in its waters. It was fed by the overflow from the King's Bath spring, which in the Southgate area was given the title of the Bum Ditch. **[fig.1], [fig.2].**

The Council Minutes of the 1790s also mention the creation of another Horse Bath. Until 2008 its position was not known, but papers recently discovered

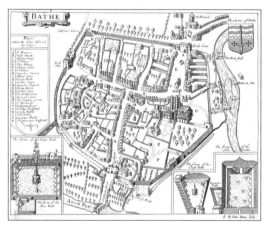

fig 1: Bathe as depicted in John Speed's Map of Somersetshire, 1610. This inset in Speed's map of the County provides a detailed plan of the City of Bath.
Bath in Time – Bath Central Library Collection

by Colin Johnston enable its site to be located precisely, more so than that of the Tudor Horse Bath - i.e. it was in the premises known as No.17 Stall Street before the modern retail block was built. These buildings, at the south-east end of the street, are popularly known as 'the Marks and Spencer block': the bath lay somewhere in the middle.

This article examines what is known and what can be conjectured about the two baths. The history of the Ham meadow, as the location of the Tudor Horse Bath was called, has been summarised in Mike Chapman's booklet[1] on the Ham and Southgate areas, the first detailed description of the locality to be

Facing: Detail from John Speed's map of Somersetshire, 1627 edition.
The Horse Bath is shown below Ham Gate, to the west of Bum Ditch.
Bath in Time – Bath Central Library Collection

published. The story of the site on which the Georgian Horse Bath stood has never been recorded. This seems an opportune moment to recount it, and the article ends with a study of the changing uses of the area, reflecting the changing tastes of each age.

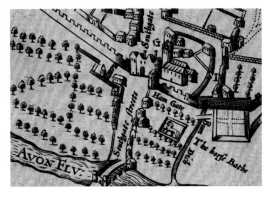

fig 2: Detail from John Speed's map of Somersetshire, 1627 edition. Showing the area to the south of the city, including Ham Gate, the Horse Bath, Bum Ditch and Southgate Street.
Bath in Time – Bath Central Library Collection

§

The Tudor Horse Bath

In the first volume of *Bath History*, Stephen Bird pointed out that in the plan of Bath inset in Speed's map of Somerset, many details of the city are correct.[2] The ruined Abbey dominates the drawing, and it seems possible that the map was created as part of the campaign to restore that church. From a long study of its contents, the Survey of Old Bath would judge that it is based on a very accurate survey of the city, correct for c.1575, though of course the Jacobean engraver has not done the justice to it that modern printing would achieve - some of the angles and other proportions are wrong. However the essence is there, and we can believe that a Tudor hot bath for horses really existed.

Speed does not give 'pases' (paces) for this map and it is therefore not one of those drawn by himself, but one which he had collected. In the old Reference Library in Queen Square it used to be catalogued as 'Girtin's map inset'. There was a later cartographer named Girtin, but the Tudor Girtin has not yet been rediscovered.

About 1575, therefore, Bath possessed something unique in Britain, a thermal bath for horses. Bath had suffered a period of decline after the Dissolution. The cloth trade was moving away from the old guild towns to the countryside - cloth factories were sometimes even set up in the sites of the despoiled monasteries. At the same time, the city had lost any income from sales or employment created by the Priory. The situation has been discussed by Dr. John Wroughton in *Tudor Bath*.[3] The city fathers set out to promote the Spa, offering the benefits of the waters even to the horse world. Presumably the idea came to them from the writings of Dr. William Turner, as quoted below - and presumably before 1567, since the Horse Bath has not been discovered in the Chamberlain's Accounts, which date from that year.[4]

In his booklet on the Ham and Southgate area of Bath, Mike Chapman points out that in 1279 the Bishop confirmed to the Prior his ownership of 'the meadow of the Ham below the wall' (*hamm* signifying water meadow).[5] The grant included 'Isabelle mulle' or Isabel mill, with a garden and the right to make two fishponds proper to the mill. Leland also mentioned that the water from the King's Bath turned a mill and then went into the Avon above Bath Bridge.[6] This suggests that Isabel Mill, if that were it, was still operating in his day.

Mike Chapman has taken the view that when the site ceased to be used as a mill, the mill-pond may have been re-used as the Horse Bath. On the diagram reproduced from the Southgate booklet a site for Isabel Mill is suggested corresponding with the possible location of Speed's Horse Bath. This also corresponds with an indentation in the eastern boundaries of the old properties along that stretch. **[fig. 3]**.

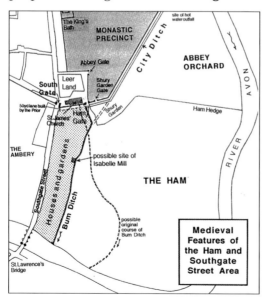

fig 3: **Medieval Features of the Ham and Southgate Street Area.** Showing the possible site for Isabelle Mill.
Illustration by Mike Chapman

John Wood stated in his *Essay* that while the construction of the Queen's Bath was in hand (in 1576), '.. a large Pond was made in a Garden upon the South Side of Saint James's Church to receive the waste Water of the King's Bath; and this was some time used as a Bath for Horses, and called the Horse Bath'.[7] Note the slightly different site. Also, it would suggest that the only outflow from the King's Bath ran eastwards and then into the Avon on the east, that it had to be stopped while the Queen's Bath was built, and that the southwards drain was a new one. However as already pointed out, Leland stated that water from the King's Bath ran southwards, and there is evidence that it did so long before him.

The Colthurst family held the Ham in the latter sixteenth century, and any cold watercourses would be included. However by that time the City considered itself to be in charge of the thermal springs, with a right to use the water as it chose. Speed's drawing actually shows the Horse Bath within the gardens of the houses alongside Southgate Street, with the name 'The Horse Bath' lying in the Ham. No surviving deed from the properties in that area mentions the Horse Bath. They date from the late sixteenth century on, and it appears that the bath did not last. Gilmore's map of 1694 does not show it. **[fig. 4].**

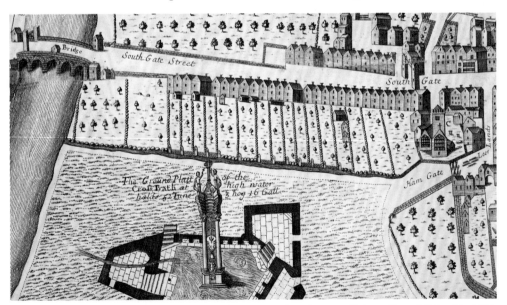

fig 4: Detail from Joseph Gilmore's map of the City of Bath, 1717. Originally published in 1694, this detail shows the privvies lining the Bum Ditch on the eastern side of Southgate Street.
Bath in Time – Bath Central Library Collection

The Georgian Horse Bath

Early in 2008 Colin Johnston discovered among the papers of the City Chamberlain some invoices and receipts dated 1793, referring to the Horse Bath of the time, which he checked with the original Council Minutes. Although the existence of a reference to the Horse Bath was known, it was not previously known whether it had actually been built. The Minutes and the new papers also made it possible to state exactly where the Horse Bath lay.

Three people are particularly mentioned – firstly Walter Wiltshire, probably the well-known carrier discussed by Dr. Brenda Buchanan. Secondly John Symons, a surgeon who as Trevor Fawcett points out in *Bath Administer'd*, had managed the baths himself for about ten years until 1787, being then replaced by a Council Committee. Thirdly, Harry Atwood, also a surgeon.[8]

There is reference to the void ground belonging to the Atwoods in Stall Street: this was the site later called No. 17 Stall Street. The invoices also included Mr. Biggs's house, and this helps make the site precise. Thomas Biggs held what was later known as No.18 Stall Street.[9] The nature of the Atwood's ground, No. 17, is more complicated, because it once consisted of two properties, both of which were held at one time by the Atwoods.

Isaac Titley, salt refiner, gathered up the three old properties at the north-west corner of our block, as well as the "Salthouse" which had been created at the east of them. This Salthouse was once held by Richard Gullidge, who also once owned the southernmost of Titley's three properties against Stalls Street. The holdings are shown in [fig. 5].

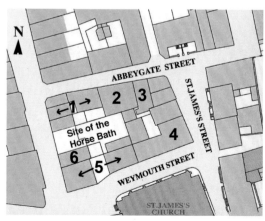

fig 5: Detail of the land north of St James's Church in Georgian times. See main text for a description for the holdings of each numbered property.
Illustration by Mike Chapman

Titley's lease of 1797 for Gullidge's old holding states that the property to the south of it, the *northern* side of No. 17, is void and the building has been taken down by the Corporation.[10] This land once belonged to the Atwoods and was mortgaged by William Chapman. William Chapman's lease of 1767 states that south of it, the *southern* part of No.17, there is void land belonging to the Atwoods, formerly to Moses Catchmore and others.[11] Thomas Biggs' lease of 1789 for No.18 states that he has void ground north of him now belonging to the Corporation.

There is therefore no doubt that when the Horse Bath was mooted, the site of No.17 Stall Street was 1) void, 2) land associated with the Atwoods, 3) next to the house of Thomas Biggs. Not surprisingly, no other site in Stall Street had these three attributes. There is therefore no doubt as to where the Georgian Horse Bath was built.

Presumably here were a couple of old properties, built after the Dissolution into the site of what was once the churchyard of St. James's Church, which had, as is said now, passed their sell-by date. There were apparently no takers for the land at the time, and there was a chance of profit from the bath. It also added to the amenities of the Spa.

Colin Johnston's discovery attracted a good deal of media attention, and the purpose of a hot bath for horses was discussed on national radio. Dr. Louise Curth, senior lecturer in Health Studies at Bath Spa University suggested that the bath was intended to have medicinal uses (as the reference to the two surgeons would suggest), as proposed in the Tudor age by Dr. William Turner. Water is often used in the management of horses, for instance wading in sea water to strengthen legs. Horses with injured limbs will swim around a heated pool, exercising their legs without placing weight on them. It may well be that the bath was intended to be therapeutic. Here it is worth quoting what Dr. Turner said in his writings on the baths:

> Furthermore because almighty God hath shapen & made herbes, stones, gummes, metalles & medicines of diverse other thinges, principally for man, it is to be thought that this will is that the same should som tyme serve such creatures of his, as man can not wel want. Wherefore as it is wel done that herbes & medecines made of diverse other thinges, should be geven unto the beastes that serve us, so I thinke that it were not amisse, if that we made the bathes after they have served man, for whom they were

principally made, serve also to help horses. For performing whereof I would wishe that one or ii.bathes in som convenient place might be drawen out from one or two of the hotest baths, and then wold I have so devised, that the horses that have diseases in the legges and joyntes, might stand in the bath almoste unto the belly, and that other that have other diseases, mighte stand hygher in the water, whych thynge maye easelye be brought to passe, if that two holes be made wyth stopholes, the one hygher, and the other lower, that a man maye set the horse as depe or shalowe as he list, the water increasinge or decreasynge accordinge to the holdinge in or lettinge out of the water.

I thinke verely that the bath of brimstone within the space of a moneth wil heale splentes, spavines, and all knobbes, hard lumpes and swellinges, if they be not verye olde, frettishinge or founderinge facies or fashones, and al such like disease that are without, if the horses by the advise of a cunning horsleche have geven them conveniente drinckes them [sic] before they come to the bath, and orden for them such emplasters and pouders as are mete for them to use in the bathynge tyme, but whylse they stande restinge them selves oute of the bathe. And my advise is that they that have not muche money to bestowe upon horsleches, that they laye in good quantite the slyme and groundes of the bathe upon the sore places of the horsses all that tyme that they are oute of the bathe, restinge them in the stable betwene one bathynge tyme and an other. But I woulde not that anye man shoulde understande me here that I woulde not that the horse should be exercised in theyr bathinge tyme, for that is not my meaninge, for I would that a horse shoulde be as well exercised as a man, and so muche more as he is stronger then a man, excepte the diseases be in his fete, and then are they more measurablye to be exercised.[12]

All the same, it is possible that grooming also played a part. Washing down working animals is traditional and still carried on overseas with buffalo and elephants. Plato mentions the hot and cold springs of Atlantis and the use of baths for cattle and horses, though he does not state whether he supposed these to be hot. Trevor Fawcett has referred to washing-places for horses in a recent article in the *Bath Magazine*, and in a private communication he has pointed out that information on these, particularly off Walcot Street and in places near the Old Bridge, is gained from newspaper reports of horses, riders, and sometimes whole coaches being swept away by the current.[13] A more convenient system would be desirable.

Trevor Fawcett points out the importance of horses and coaching in the infrastructure of the time. Horses were pastured outside the city, sometimes as far south as Widcombe and Lyncombe. They may have been washed down before being led through the South Gate. The location of many coaching inns in the district concerned is known.

Opposite the site of the bath lay the Lamb Inn, famous as a coaching inn (not the later Lamb which used once to be called the Mermaid). On the south side of the Lamb was the Royal Oak. Towards the north-west end of Stall Street was the famous White Hart mentioned later by Jane Austen and Dickens. The Beare lay at the north end of Stall Street, soon to be replaced by Union Street. On the east side of Stall Street, on the site which is now the south-western corner of York Street, stood the ancient Three Tuns, rebuilt when York Street was created. It possessed extensive stabling, sites later cut through by Swallow Street.

The diagram shows how the thermal water may have run southwards from the King's Bath to be available for the new Horse Bath. The basic property

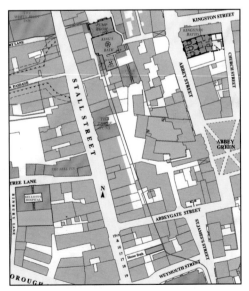

fig 6: Detail of buildings in the Stall Street area of Bath in Georgian times. The possible route of thermal water is traced running from the King's Bath parallel to Stall Street, to the Horse Bath.

Illustration by Mike Chapman after Peter Davenport

outlines in this plan have been taken from the late eighteenth century map in the Survey's *The Spa Quarter of Bath,* commissioned by the Spa Project Team and drawn by Mike Chapman.[14] The route of the water has been adapted from Peter Davenport, *Medieval Bath Uncovered*.[15] Part of a thermal channel was discovered during excavations by Bath Archaeological Trust, confirming the flow of water southwards as described by Leland. Presumably the channel was originally created by Bishop John de Villula to run parallel to the western perimeter wall of his palace enclave, the palace being the subject of the Trust's excavation.

The water is shown running away south-eastwards so as to join with the Ham Gate and then flow southwards to the river. Even if it did not follow this line originally, it would have had to be redirected when St. James's Church was built (1279). Where it enters the block of property in which the Horse Bath was situated, it crosses the site of the Salthouse, and may have been useful in running that workshop. **[fig. 6].**

§

New evidence

The new evidence discovered in the city archives by Colin Johnston is as follows. Firstly, the Council Minutes: February 6th 1793

> 14th To take into Consideration the Expediency and Utility of making a Hot Bath for Horses with Suitable Conveniences thereto on the Void Piece of Ground on the East Side of Stall Street in this City lately belonging to John Atwood and to Resolve what is fit and ought to be done therein. -
> A Plan & Elevation for a Horse Bath on the East side of Stall Street in this City with Suitable Conveniences thereto with an Estimate of the Expences attending the making the same being now produced and taken into Consideration and thought useful *Therefore Resolved* that the same be and is hereby approved and ordered to be carryed into Execution under the direction of the Mayor Justices and Chamberlain of this City for the time being together with Walter Wiltshire Esqr. Mr. John Symons and Mr. Harry Atwood or any three of them who are hereby made a Committee for that Purpose.[16]

The Plan and Elevation have not so far been forthcoming. Unfortunately key diagrams are often missing, as if some collector's hand has been at work. Presumably there was a ramp at each end leading in and out of the water, and a walkway at the side for attendants. Unless an invoice is missing, there seem to have been no railings, as ironwork is not mentioned.

The existence of the invoices and receipts confirms that the work was actually done. The heading of the first to be considered[17] is unclear. It includes the date March 14th 1793, although the account itself runs to April 30th. The text runs: 'The Copration [sic] of the City of Bath March 14. 1793 Dr. To Jno. Fisher to puling [sic] Down wall Removing & filling the Old Stone from ye.Horse Bath'. This must refer to old stonework on the site, since the Tudor Horse Bath had disappeared long before.

The list begins with an undated entry, presumably referring to March 14th itself, for 1 man for 1 day's work for pulling down the wall, 1/6d. It continues with entries for carts for hauling and men for filling. Later on April 25th there were two carts and men hauling rubbish that came out of the 'Schore', i.e. sewer, for 17/- - carts were evidently expensive.

The total amount owing on this account was £10.5.6 to which was added '£33.16.11' referring to the total from another paper, making in all £44.2.5. The names J. Symons and A.M. Mayor appear at the bottom.

A second paper states that it is for digging and removing the earth from the foundation of the Horse Bath in Stall Street, from March 14th to May 18th 1793. It cites the sum of £33.16.11, for digging and carting away as per agreement, and adds in the other bill of £10.5.6. There follows a receipt for the total of the two bills, at £44.2.5 with fivepence deducted , at £44.2.0, 'Received … by me Jno. Fisher'.

Another and much clearer invoice[18] is for sums owing to Walter Harris and Samuel Wallop, headed 'for Masons & Labourers Work at the Horse Bath & Biggs's House adjoining' - dated 'Beginning April 9th and ending May 7th 1793', and covering 'Ground Pining Walls Digging & Making a Sewer etc'. Mortar boys are charged at 8d.a day, masons' boys 1/2d., labourers 1/8d., the masons 2/6d. and Mr. Harris himself 3/-.

Supplies include lime, gripps, two baskets, and candles. There is also beer, a necessary part of accounts, at l0d. The total is £9.6.7. This time the paper ends with the names of Thos. Chantry and A.M. Mayor. Once again there is a receipt, signed by Walter Harris. Again it has been discounted: the sum of 5/3d. has been removed (as noted on the bill itself) and Harris gets £9.1.4.

These six items - one reference in the Council Minutes, three invoices and two receipts - comprise all that is known about the creation of the Georgian Horse Bath. The deeds held at the Record Office enable its site to be shown as the later No. 17 Stall Street. In 1802 Richard Cruttwell made a bid for the land. His new lease referring to his new buildings[19] is dated 1807 and the life of the bath was evidently short.

§

The History of the Sites

The history of the sites is interesting as indicating the kind of spot where a bath for horses might be built. The Tudor Horse Bath was in an area which had always traditionally been open land used for grazing south of the city walls. *Hamm* signifies 'Water meadow', as already mentioned. Mike Chapman's booklet on the Ham and Southgate areas outlined what is known about this district, and can be referred to where further background material is of interest.

The Tudor Horse Bath will have arisen naturally out of the visible flow of hot water on the site, combined with the efforts of the City fathers to promote the Spa, and Dr. William Turner's suggestions. The Georgian Horse Bath again was naturally part of the promotion of the Spa, in this case with the opportunist use of an empty site.

John de Villula's Bishop's Palace, apparently in use by 1106, seems to have had no housing against its western perimeter wall, but probably a grassy bank grazed on by geese and goats. The road running past it was still called "the way from Stalls Street to the South Gate". By the end of the thirteenth century the Bishops had effectively ceased to live in Bath, and they began granting out building plots, including the land against their western wall. At about the same time, they caused the old Church of St. James's (wherever it had previously been sited, on which there are different interpretations) to be moved to the southern part of the area now called popularly 'the Marks and Spencer block'.

The whole area of this block was once a close belonging to the De Gournay family, with a piece by the South Gate belonging to the rector of the church of 'Chiw'. It was typical of great families to invest in a site within a walled city. No mention of a house on the close is made in the two known deeds, but presumably there was one.[20] The family could retreat there in turbulent times if need be, and at other times it was an investment (other such examples can be given from the early deeds of Bath). On the other hand, if the city was besieged, there was a military family to hold the gate.

The land was ceded to the Bishop and a small church was built.[21] As far as we have any information the rest of the block originally acted as a churchyard, with a route to the Abbey Gate across the north, and a route down the eastern side from the Abbey Gate to the new Ham Gate, this part being the site of the later St. James's Street South. The whole area was known as Leere (or Leer) Land, or Leare Land.

'Leere land' was the property of a church. As the name lingered on, we do presume that this remained the churchyard of St. James's during the later Middle Ages, though some postulate that it was built on then. We suppose that some buildings appeared against the churchyard walls, along the route which now also began to be known as Stalls Street. By the end of the sixteenth century, part of the churchyard had certainly been taken over. Protestants did not have the same use for extensive church property as the Catholic Church.

Early secular plots on the north side of the churchyard ran right through to the route then called Leere Land or Leere Lane, with the main buildings presumably all at the western end alongside the street. People did not care to live on ancient graveyards and tested them out with gardens and stables. If too many apparitions did not disturb the livestock, they would begin to build housing. Eventually most of the site was divided up, leaving St. James's Church with only a small churchyard and a route through to it from Stalls Street (apparently the lane called Mortality Alley in John Wood's time).

By the time of the Survey of 1641 the site had adapted itself to the Spa and its visitors. Inside the gate, the land of 'Chiw' had evidently become at least part of the site of 'one wood barton called Tenyseplay'. St. James's Church still remained, where one could pause for prayer. North of it, occupying a large part of the site, with stables to the east, was the Golden Lyon. North of that were the holdings of tradesmen.

In the eighteenth century, St. James's Church was enlarged more than once. As fashion moved to the new crescents and terraces, parts of old Bath became more derelict, on the one hand, or more industrialised on the other. If

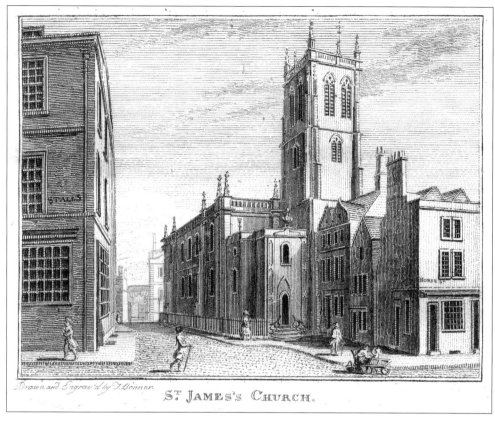

fig 7: St. James's Church, 1784. Close to the site of the Horse Bath, see fig 5. Drawn and engraved by T. Bonnor, 10 March 1784. Note that Horse Street (recorded on the right-hand building) became Southgate Street in the 1820s.
Bath in Time – Bath Central Library Collection

we review the area in the days of the Horse Bath, it is hardly a smart district. Buildings still stood at the west end of the church where the tennis court had once been erected. They were cleared away when the tower of St. James's was enlarged again. North of the church Weymouth Street had already appeared by 1778. **[fig.7]**.

North of the church, we can see the layout of the times on an enlarged section of the Survey's map already used above to illustrate the possible route of thermal water to the Horse Bath **[fig. 5]**. 5: 1 indicates the properties already referred to, belonging to Isaac Titley, salt refiner. 5: 2 indicates the Salthouse itself. 5: 3 is the Talbot Inn, which later spilt over to the east, as shown in a later drawing. Cruttwell held most of the eastern side: 5: 4 is the Printing House. A very fine elevation of this exists in Bath Central Library Collections. The two executors of the original Richard Cruttwell, i.e. William Matthewes and Richard Shuttleworth Cruttwell, held it by lease of 1800. 5: 5 was once part of the Golden Lyon. In 1774 the Atwoods held it, at which date it was already no longer the Golden Lyon. The Atwoods were braziers, and a workshop is marked on their plan. By 1778 it was leased to Dafter, who held the mortgage, and in 1804 to Henry Griffith, currier. The building was later called 19 Stall Street. 5: 6 is 18 Stall Street, Thomas Biggs's house. The void ground is the site of the Horse Bath. Biggs held No. 18 by lease of 1789. By 1821 Griffith leased it, with a William Biggs, vendor of newspapers, as one of the lives.[22]

To summarise, our first information on the site is that it was held by the De Gournays, one of the great families. It then became a religious venue, and the block was for long a churchyard. The Spa then crept in, with the Golden Lyon and its stabling and inn accommodation. By the late eighteenth century we find industry typical of the dawning Industrial Revolution. Nowadays it is the site of retail outlets.

In 1802 Richard Shuttleworth Cruttwell bid for the land of No. 17. By his lease of April 20th 1807, he had built a stone and timber messuage with suitable offices, with the front set back so as to widen Stall Street. The area continued in much the same pattern until the bombing of the Second World War, when St. James's Church was burnt out in 1942. The church was finally demolished in 1957. It was decided to redevelop the whole area, including St. James's Street South and Weymouth House. Part of Weymouth House had already been demolished to create the rotunda used for the National Schools. Some picturesque houses were included in the final demolition, some of which were mentioned in Adam Fergusson's *The Sack of Bath*.[23] The new development block, completed in 1961, included the Marks and Spencer building by the architects Munro and Partners, considered in Pevsner as 'one of the better postwar commercial buildings in this part of the town', and the (former) Woolworth building by W.B. Brown.[24] [fig. 8].

The modern retail block was a great success, providing many happy shopping hours. It can be seen in the illustration, across the Southgate development site. Looking at it, the spectator would naturally never guess its history. There is no sign of St. James's Church, nor the De Gournay's close

fig 8: View of Bath from Beechen Cliff, March 1972. The neo-Georgian Woolworth block of 1961 was built on the site of St. James's Church. The old Southgate area is shown cleared prior to building the previous Southgate Shopping Centre.
Bath in Time – Photograph by Snowdon

which preceded it. The Golden Lyon has vanished, and the later Talbot, the Atwood's works and Cruttwell's printing works. It is only in 2008 that it has even been realised that the Georgian Horse Bath once lay there.

Notes

1. Mike Chapman, *An Historical Guide to the Ham and Southgate Area of Bath* (The Survey of Old Bath, 1997), *passim*.
2. Stephen Bird, 'The Earliest Map of Bath', *Bath History Vol.I* (Alan Sutton, 1986), p.145.
3. John Wroughton, *Tudor Bath, Life and Strife in the Little City 1485-1603* (The Lansdown Press, 2006), pp.38 ff, 'Decline in the Economy'.
4. F.D. Wardle, 'The Accounts of the Chamberlains of the City of Bath 1568-1602', *Somerset Record Society Vol.38*, 1923.
5. W. Hunt, 'Two Chartularies of Bath Priory', *Somerset Record Society Vol.7*, 1893, ii, 808.
6. L. Toulmin Smith ed., *The Itinerary of John Leland in or about the years 1535-1543* (1907), part.II, p.142.
7. John Wood, *An Essay toward a Description of Bath*, 1765 edition, p.207.
8. Walter Wiltshire: cf. Dr. Brenda Buchanan, 'Walter Wiltshire', *Oxford Dictionary of National Biography* (OUP, 2004).
   John Symons: cf. Trevor Fawcett, *Bath Administer'd, Corporation Affairs at the 18th-Century Spa* (Ruton, 2001), p.15, under 'Baths and Pump Rooms'.
   Harry Atwood: a connection of the Chapman family named as a surgeon on Corporation leases. Cf. BC/152/2362 (Furman's *Repertory*). Lease of June 27th 1766, in the Sawclose, to Harry Atwood surgeon and Elizabeth Atwood spinster.
9. Bath Record Office, BC/153/3376/1/4. Lease of November 23rd 1789 to Mr. Thomas Biggs, yeoman. With plan. '..bounded on the North by Void Ground…'. This lease should actually be under section 3 of the deed packet.
10. BRO, BC/153/3376/1/6. Lease of July 10th 1797 to Isaac Titley. With plan. 'bounded … on the South by Void Ground on which a messuage some time past stood … demised … to William Chapman but which demise is expired or surrendered and the Messuage taken down …'.
11. BRO, BC/152/2389 (Furman's *Repertory*). Lease of July 13th 1767 to William Chapman of Lyncombe and Widcombe, gentleman (i.e. William Chapman, alderman and mayor, illustrated on p.32 of the *Survey of Bath and District, No. 22*, October 2007. Owner of Lyncombe Farm, now called Lyncombe Hall). 'a Tenement formerly of Moses Catchmore and others now a Void Piece of Ground belonging to Messrs. Atwood's on the Southside … now in possession of [i.e. the

main property itself] John Atwood and James Atwood …'. Cruttwell's lease of April 20th 1807 states that William Chapman held a mortgage on this property (see note 19).

12. Dr. William Turner, *A book of the natures and properties of the baths of England*, (1562).

13. Trevor Fawcett, 'Georgian Horsepower', *The Bath Magazine, Issue 16* (MC Publishing Ltd., June 2008), p.42. Letter to Elizabeth Holland, in 'Correspondence', *The Survey of Bath and District, No. 23*, (The Survey of Old Bath, October 2008).

14. Giles White (Project editor), Mike Chapman and Elizabeth Holland, *The Spa Quarter of Bath, A History in Maps* (Survey of Old Bath for the Bath Spa Project, 2005), 'Spa Sites in Bath in the Early 1770s', p.13.

15. Peter Davenport, *Medieval Bath Uncovered* (Tempus, 2002), illus.60, p.136.

16. BRO, Council Minute Book No. 11, February 6th 1793, p.441.

17. BRO, Corporation Vouchers/1793/219 (two invoices and receipt).

18. BRO, Corporation Vouchers/1793/178 (invoices and receipt).

19. BRO, BC/153/3376/2/1. Lease of April 20th 1807 to Richard Shuttleworth Cruttwell. With plan, showing the six feet the property has been set back fronting Stall Street. A plot of ground with newly erected and built at his own costs a Stone and Timber Messuage. Refers back to William Chapman's lease of 1767.

20. BL Egerton MSS 3316 fol.62r.

21   PRO Charter Rolls 8 Ed.I., m12.

22. Details of all the leases in this summary can be found in the Record Office's website. Reference number for deed packets – BC/153.

23. Adam Fergusson, *The Sack of Bath, a record and an indictment* (Compton Russell, 1973). Cf.pp.24-25.

24. Michael Forsyth, *Pevsner Architectural Guides: Bath* (Yale University Press, 2003), p.114.

The Crescent as it Might Have Been

Katharine Wall

In April 2008, the exhibition 'Bath As It Might Have Been' opened at the Victoria Art Gallery. This showcased prints, plans and watercolours from the Council's collections, illustrating architects' and planners' unrealised ideas for improving Bath, from the mid-eighteenth to the late-twentieth centuries. The exhibition covered a wide range of proposals, from an early nineteenth-century design for a monument the size of Nelson's Column in Laura Place, and one from the 1890s for roofing over the newly-discovered Great Bath, to the infamous 1965 Buchanan Plan, which promised to end traffic congestion in Bath, by sending cars through a tunnel underneath the city centre. Each of the exhibits in 'Bath As It Might Have Been' has a story to tell about the aspirations of its era, the ambitions of Bath architects, and what people in the past felt was needed to turn Bath into a better, more prosperous and beautiful city. This article focuses on just a few of the pieces included in the exhibition: Those that relate to one of Bath's most famous and best loved landmarks, the Royal Crescent.

The story of the Royal Crescent has been so thoroughly and so often covered elsewhere that all that is needed here are the most basic facts. Constructed between 1767 and 1775, the Crescent was designed by John Wood the Younger. It may well, however, have been loosely based on the ideas of John Wood the Elder, given the hint of paganism suggested by in its moon-inspired name and, as with the approach the elder Wood developed from Queen Square onwards, the treatment of a terrace of houses as a grand, palatial unit. As with Wood the Elder's landmark constructions, the Royal Crescent was conceived very much as a whole, and it was vital to the architect that the appearance of structural unity was not to be interfered with. Even though the individual houses were constructed by different builders, strict adherence to Wood's conception was enforced through sub-clauses in the lease for each plot, committing them to execute the elevation strictly to Wood's design. Furthermore the sub-clauses stipulated that, once finished, the façades 'shall not...at any time or times afterwards be ever altered or varied'. It was clear that John Wood the Younger wanted the Royal Crescent to survive intact far into the future.

Facing: Detail of proposed improvements to the Royal Crescent, c.1850.
Fountains, railings and balustrade were proposed by the Victorians to
enhance the landscape in front of the Crescent.
Bath in Time – Bath Central Library Collection

Of the proposals to be looked at here, only one comes close to entirely disregarding Wood's wishes, in threatening radical changes to the Royal Crescent. This scheme is vividly illustrated in one of the most striking exhibits in 'Bath As It Might Have Been', a watercolour from 1945, illustrating an audacious proposal to turn the Crescent into a new Civic Centre for Bath. This was just a small part of a large much larger, citywide scheme, the *Plan for Bath*.[1] Commissioned by Bath City Council, the Plan sought to provide a framework for the redevelopment and modernisation of Bath in the post-World War II period. Its stated aim was 'rejuvenation with a firm hand' for areas devastated by the Bath Blitz. The city centre was to be redesigned on a more rational, 'zoned' basis, with, for example, separate areas for shopping, 'health', business and light industry. This scheme was masterminded by Patrick Abercrombie, a planner of national standing, brought in as a consultant, but the details were filled in by two Bath City Council employees, Town Planning Officer Henry Anthony Mealand, and City Engineer John Owens. The planner of choice during the 1940s, Abercrombie undertook projects to piece back together various war-torn towns including Plymouth, Hull and Bournemouth. He knew Bath well, having been involved in planning for the city since 1928, and seems to have been a figure who cut quite a dash: *The Bath Chronicle and Herald* memorably described him as 'slim and vivid' and 'a cross between Sir Christopher Wren and Walt Disney'.[2]

The *Plan for Bath* laid claim to the ambition to restore and protect Bath's important buildings by creating a traffic-free city centre, but this was to be achieved at a price, higher than just the redevelopment and change of use of existing buildings: Whole streets of Georgian buildings were to be demolished to make way for modern developments such as shopping precincts, a new Bath College and a much enlarged Mineral Water Hospital. True to the spirit of the *Plan for Bath*, its proposal for the Royal Crescent was radical. The central sixteen houses were to be converted into a new civic centre for Bath; they were in effect to become one single property, with a large new block added on behind to accommodate a suitably imposing Council chamber. **[fig.1]** It was noted that the Guildhall was too small to house all of the necessary Council departments (and also that music from the Parade Gardens bandstand was distracting Council staff from their duties!) Abercrombie, Mealand and Owens may have privately felt that redeveloping the Royal Crescent was the ideal way to make a big and very public statement of their radical vision for Bath, but publicly, they

fig 1: The proposed new Council Chamber and Committee Rooms at the rear of the Royal Crescent, 1945. The proposed east-west route through Bath passes past the spire-less St Andrew's Church and the forecourt to this unlikely development.
Victoria Art Gallery – Bath & North East Somerset Council

were careful to provide detailed justification for the proposal on architectural and well as practical grounds, with the published Plan proclaiming:

> 'The dilapidated Mews which fringe the site do injustice to this finest creation of Wood. The sweeping away of these would provide a site for a Council Chamber and ancillary rooms as an annexe linked with the Crescent [and] set within spacious gardens …The existing elevations would remain and the unbalanced and unsightly appendages which have been added could be replaced by properly grouped and positioned sanitary annexes. At the same time the main cornices, lines and fenestration of the rear elevation could be restored in such a manner as to harmonise with the buildings

comprising the new Council Chamber. ….for the convenience of ratepayers a single office, representative of every Corporation department, would be established; at this office enquiries or complaints could be made, rates and other accounts paid, and attached to it there would be an Information Bureau where enquiries could be made as to road, rail or air travel, also spa and other activities of the City. The transfer of civic administration to the Crescent could be very conveniently accomplished, and the development of this great Crescent as a Centre of Local Government would create one of the finest civic centres in the country. It would be a bold scheme calling for wisdom and great courage.'[3] **[fig 2].**

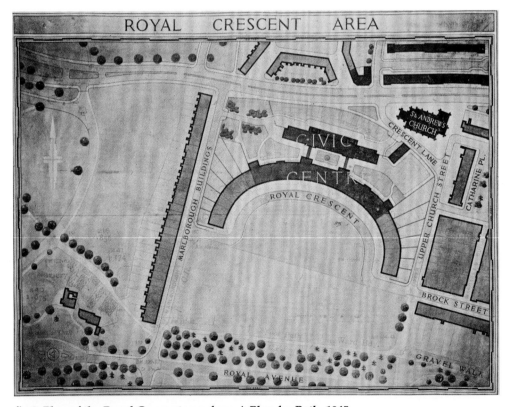

fig 2: Plan of the Royal Crescent area from A Plan for Bath, 1945.
The highlighted area in the centre shows the proposed centre of Civic Administration.
Bath in Time – Bath Central Library Collection

The *Plan for Bath* was, on the whole, enthusiastically received. At first, little was made of the proposal for the Crescent, and it seemed that people barely noticed it amongst the excitement over the Plan as a whole. The promise of a city with every modern facility, an excellent road system and all traces of bomb damage removed had great appeal to the war-weary people of Bath. A public relations exercise, seeking both to publicise the proposals and test reactions to the Plan, was carried out through an exhibition at the Victoria Art Gallery during February 1945. **[fig. 3].** Artists' impressions of the proposed new roads and buildings were put on display, together with a huge wooden model of the

fig 3: The opening of the exhibition for A Plan for Bath, Feb. 1945. The Minister of Town and Country Planning, the Right Hon. W. S. Morrison, M.P. M.C, opens the exhibition at the Victoria Art Gallery.
Bath in Time – Bath Central Library Collection

redeveloped city centre. The exhibition brochure made the *Plan for Bath's* attitude to historic buildings explicit, proclaiming: 'Preservation without economic usefulness would be prohibitive in cost and would make Bath a museum. Fortunately most of the Georgian buildings can be adapted to modern uses justifying preservation and restoration.'[4] Unsurprisingly, the exhibition generated enormous public interest, with up to two thousand people a day crowding in to view the proposals (in an era when the Gallery's normal daily attendance rarely exceeded two hundred). For the duration of the exhibition the pages of *The Bath Chronicle and Herald* were full of articles about the Plan. Most were tinged with admiration for Abercrombie's daring and visionary proposals, almost as if the local press was wary of seeming to throw cold water on Bath's glittering future. The paper's letters pages, too, were dominated by enthusiastic comment on the Plan, with only the occasional voice objecting to the proposals for the Royal Crescent. An A. Collins of Newbridge Road fumed: 'That part of the plan dealing with the Royal Crescent is outrageous... to turn it into municipal offices so that the officials can entertain their friends and relations in lordly surroundings is unthinkable... it is up to the citizens of Bath to prevent squandering and an orgy of vandalism.'[5] However, it seems that the Plan's projected huge expense and complexity of implementation, far above any belief that the integrity of historic buildings should be respected, became its downfall. Councillor Huntley, writing in *The Bath Chronicle and Herald*, claimed that: 'The Bath public has, for the last three weeks, been gazing into the future, hypnotised by this beautiful bubble. They see it, an airy-fairy bubble floating over their heads, and they are inclined to forget the more matter-of-fact business of rates and taxes.'[6] Once the *Plan for Bath* exhibition had closed and the associated excitement began to subside, councillors began a detailed examination of the proposals. In October 1945, Bath City Council formally adopted a reduced version of the *Plan for Bath*. Fortunately, the conversion of the Royal Crescent into a civic centre was one of the first parts of the scheme to be decisively rejected by local politicians.

The *Plan for Bath* proposed radical changes not just to the Royal Crescent itself, but also to the roads around it. The A4 was to be rerouted as a dual carriageway running just behind the Royal Crescent, along Julian Road. Patrick Abercrombie always gave the creation of a modern, coherent road system the highest priority in his town plans; in Bath, with its Georgian streets and hilly surrounding area, this was a particular challenge. Abercrombie felt that re-routing Bath's main east-west road behind the Crescent had several advantages: it offered a way to bypass the city centre, freeing it from heavy traffic; also it was one of very few possible ways to turn the A4 into a wide, modern road capable of coping with projected increases in traffic levels. Furthermore, as more people (and thus traffic) would need to travel to the Royal Crescent in its new capacity as the civic centre, this enlarged road would ease access. As with the proposal for the Crescent itself, a considerable price was to be paid for these 'improvements': Many of the Georgian houses along the route were to be demolished in order to free up sufficient space to widen Julian Road into a dual carriageway. **[fig. 4].** Lansdown Road would have undergone major changes, with a tunnel dug underneath it to connect Julian Road with the London Road. The civil engineering work needed to achieve this would have been enormous and expensive, and so it is hardly surprising that Abercrombie's plans for Julian Road did not go ahead.

Other exhibits from *Bath As It Might Have Been* looked at proposals to alter

fig 4: The Proposed East-West Route (Julian Road) passing under Lansdown Road, 1945. Included in Abercrombie's A Plan for Bath, this radical solution was a bold attempt to solve Bath's growing traffic congestion.
Bath in Time – Bath Central Library Collection

the Royal Crescent's surroundings. An engraving from 1810 illustrates a scheme to improve the view from the Crescent, perhaps indicating that residents at that time felt that the area could do with some smartening-up. At this time, Crescent Fields stretched all the way down to the (Upper) Bristol Road. As the name suggests, the area was pasture, rather than the formal park that we have now. Due to legal restrictions, there had been no development on the northern side of the Bristol Road, but the southern side was lined with a higgledy-piggledy mixture of mostly utilitarian buildings in a variety of styles. It was most unlike the smart, uniform terraces that had become characteristic of Bath. This print illustrates a proposal to build a new terrace along the northern side of the Bristol Road, in the area now occupied by Crescent Gardens. The rationale offered for this was not to provide housing or make money for developers, but instead to 'improve' the view from the Crescent by hiding the existing buildings on the southern side of the road. The print illustrates the improvements most imaginatively, with a strip of paper fastened down on one side that can be put down and then folded back to cunningly reveal the 'before' and 'after' effects of the new development. Text above the moveable strip reads:

> 'These two sketches are intended to shew: First the view from the Crescent as it now appears, with the existing irregular old buildings and secondly to shew that if a line of handsome

buildings were erected as proposed they would hide nothing from the Crescent but the present ugly and irregular buildings and not impede the view from thence of all the interesting part of the Landscape which would be seen over them.' **[fig. 5]**

The strip shows an extremely long and almost featureless terrace of identical townhouses. Unfortunately, the print does not include the normal details of authorship or even of the publisher and thus gives no indication as to who was behind this plan. The repetitious and dull quality of the proposed buildings suggests that this individual was not an architect. As the development did not go ahead, one wonders if the print backfired on the scheme, as it simply showed how dull the view would become if a line of plain townhouses were to be built along the Bristol Road. The unimaginative design of the planned development was not the only obstacle that prevented this proposal going ahead: The land belonged to Lady Rivers, who was not behind the proposal and presumably had little or no enthusiasm for it. Furthermore, legal restrictions had been placed on the Crescent Fields, stipulating that the

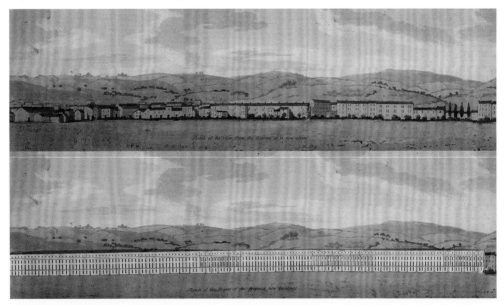

fig 5: Plan of Proposed Improvements on the lower part of the Crescent Fields in front of The Royal Crescent, 1810. Shown together, the top image displays the current view, the overlaid lower image the proposed improvements in the same setting.
Bath in Time – Bath Central Library Collection

land had to be used for pasture. The area was absolutely not available for building on, however much the Crescent's residents may have wished for a better view. The obstacles to this scheme were thus considerable, and it took almost a century for them to be overcome and the area to be developed.

Another proposal to enhance the view from the Royal Crescent is illustrated in a mid-nineteenth century lithograph by local artist, Charles James Maggs. This is a very typically Victorian plan to adorn the grass in front of the Crescent with fountains, flowerbeds and railings. **[fig. 6].** Victoria Park had opened in 1830, and this proposal was probably an attempt to bring the two parts of the park together by transforming Crescent Fields from rough, raw pastureland into a proper, formally laid-out park. The Crescent's iron railings were to be replaced by an elaborate stone balustrade. Two huge fountains were to be built, with wide basins held up by unusually large putti and water shooting so high into the air that the print shows it partially obscuring the view of the Crescent. The ha-ha, built in the 1770s to keep the livestock that grazed on Crescent Fields a comfortable distance from the houses, was to be hidden by a hedge, except for in the centre, where steps were to carry a broad path all the way from Royal Avenue

fig 6: The Royal Crescent c.1850. With the proposed Victorian embellishments. Designed by J. Maggs and drawn on stone by Chs. J. Maggs.
Bath in Time – Bath Central Library Collection

to the area immediately in front of the Crescent. Expanses of lawn were to be punctuated at regular intervals by flowerbeds and shrubs. The simplicity of the grassy space in front of the Royal Crescent was to be replaced with a park full of eye-catching features. With typical Victorian confidence the print was titled 'The Royal Crescent with the Proposed Improvements and Fountains', as if there was no possibility that the alterations could have been inappropriate.

The print gives no clue that the two fountains proposed for the Crescent lawn were just a small element in a much larger scheme for fountains across Bath. This remarkable plan has been examined in detail elsewhere.[7] Briefly, a network of fountains were proposed, stretching from St James's Square via the Royal Crescent, the Circus and Queen Square, and finishing in Laura Place. The fountains were to be connected together and fed with their own water supply, independent of the one that fed Bath's homes and businesses. It was envisaged that the water could be sourced from springs in Lansdown and would then run from one fountain to the next in sequence, with gravity keeping the supply running and the fountains playing. Unsurprisingly, the water supply was not up to the task. The scheme was thus scaled down to a single fountain in Laura Place. Once again, it was not the questioning of architectural taste and appropriateness that put paid to a scheme to alter the Royal Crescent, but practical matters instead.

Perhaps the most intriguing image of a different Royal Crescent is one that, sadly, we know the least about. This is a small pencil sketch in the Victoria Art Gallery's collection showing a curving terrace of Georgian townhouses. It is inscribed (clearly by the hand that produced the image) 'New Crescent'. The shape of the buildings and topography mark the houses in the drawing out as the Royal Crescent, but there was one significant difference - the house in the centre of the building is adorned with a classical portico. [fig. 7]. True to the conventions of Palladian architecture, the portico in this sketch emphasises the symmetry of the Crescent, and is the type of adornment that a structure of this kind would be likely to have. This little sketch reminds us how odd it is that the central house in the Royal Crescent, as built, is understated as a centrepiece, plain and almost undifferentiated from its fellows. This rather mysterious drawing has traditionally been ascribed to John Wood the Younger, but unfortunately there is no actual evidence to back up this attribution. The sketch was donated to the Gallery in 1923, part of a large bequest of local material from the Bath collector, A.W. Page. He believed the drawing to be by Wood, and in the absence of any evidence to the contrary, the attribution has stuck,

fig 7: Pencil sketch of the 'New Crescent' with alternative central feature.
Traditionally attributed to John Wood the Younger, the central part of the Crescent includes a classical portico.
Victoria Art Gallery – Bath & North East Somerset Council

albeit tentatively. There is no knowing whether this really is a rare sketch by Wood the Younger. If it were, this would be a most remarkable find. However, putting the question of attribution aside, it shows a design that clearly works well and follows the conventions of Palladian architecture. It would be odd indeed if Wood had not considered putting a portico like the one shown on this sketch at the central part of his crescent. This mysterious little drawing serves as a reminder that this iconic Bath landmark could well have looked very different – even without the subsequent ham-fisted attempts to adapt and 'improve' the Royal Crescent in the nineteenth and twentieth centuries.

Notes

1. See Robin Lambert, 'Patrick Abercrombie and Planning in Bath', *Bath History* vol.VIII for fuller details of the Plan for Bath and Abercrombie's work for the city.
2. *The Bath Chronicle and Herald*, February 1st 1945, p.4.
3. P.Abercrombie, J.Owens and H.A.Mealand, *A Plan for Bath* (Bath, 1945), pp.55-56.
4. *A Plan for Bath* exhibition brochure, Bath City Council, 1945
5. *The Bath Chronicle and Herald*, February 13th 1945.
6. *The Bath Chronicle and Herald*, February 24th 1945.
7. M.Chapman, 'Bath and the Ornamental Public Fountain', *The Survey of Bath and District* No.22 (2007), pp.45-53.

James and George Norman and the rise of the Casualty Hospital, 1783-1861

Jan Chivers

Introduction

The amount of building work being undertaken in Bath in the eighteenth century caused problems for the Poor Law authorities because of the number of migrant workers who were not settled in city parishes. Extensive building work led to increasing numbers of accidents involving day labourers who then, unable to work, became a drain on the poor rates or had to be removed to their parish of settlement. In order to alleviate the situation, a group of men met together, in 1787, and agreed to form a hospital, the sole purpose of which was to treat victims of serious accidents. The development of the hospital had a number of advantages not only for the poor, but also for the medical profession in Bath and, more specifically, for the two surgeons most closely associated with the hospital – James Norman and his son, George.

The medical profession was not always well regarded in the eighteenth century. Writing about medical men, Barbara Brandon Schnorrenberg wrote that the public deemed the medical profession to be more interested in making money and in quarrelling within its own membership than in curing the sick.[1] Ben Wilson, in *Decency and Disorder, 1789-1837*, described contemporary perceptions of physicians as men who were remote, expensive, possibly badly educated and often unable to offer any form of relief from suffering.[2] Medical men in Bath also had a reputation, whether deserved or not, for avarice and 'cronyism.' Robert Southey, writing in 1803, referred to Bath as 'the Canaan of Physicians', as the city was 'overstocked' with medical men and abounded with wealthy patients only too happy to have whatever disease was suggested to them.[3] In addition, Roy Porter has drawn attention to the eighteenth century as 'a golden age of quackery' and Bath, as a city devoted to healthcare and patronised by the wealthy, no doubt had more than its fair share.[4] Samuel Solomon, a well-known figure at the end of the eighteenth century whose

Facing: Detail of Portrait of George Norman FRCS 1840.
Printed and engraved by W O Geller. Published London by
Henry Benham Oct 16th 1840.
Bath in Time – Bath Central Library Collection

cure-all, the Balm of Gilead, made him a fortune, visited Bath at least twice, once in 1798 when he gave three guineas to the General Hospital and three guineas to the City Infirmary, and again in 1799 when he held consultations at 2 Queen Square.[5] Bath physicians were also satirised by both Smollett and Christopher Anstey.[6] By way of contrast, Schnorrenberg has drawn our attention to the number of reputable medical men in Bath and it is firmly in this group that James and George Norman stood.[7]

By tracing the development of the hospital and examining the career of George Norman, in particular, we are able to see how involvement with a charity enabled men to progress both professionally and socially. This article will, therefore, look closely at the development of the Casualty Hospital and at the lives of James and George Norman and will touch on the wider implications of their work within the framework of a medical charity.

§

Subscription philanthropy

By the eighteenth century it was suspected that a number of ancient charities in England had been mismanaged and that, possibly, large sums of money originally intended as charitable benefactions, had been lost. Charitable works by public subscription, based on the concepts governing joint-stock companies, therefore became the preferred method of financing such works. Bath's visitors and residents would have been familiar with the use of subscriptions for charitable causes. The first beneficiaries of this new form of philanthropy were general or accident hospitals. In London, the Public Infirmary (later the Westminster Hospital) was established in 1719, St. George's in 1733, the London in 1743 and the Middlesex in 1745.[8] Although a General Infirmary was established in Bath in 1739, it was not available to Bath residents, and it was another fifty years until the foundation of the Casualty Hospital meant that the poor in Bath were able to avail themselves of an accident hospital.[9]

The new subscription form of philanthropy had the advantage of enabling subscribers to see exactly how their money was being used, and, if they wished, to have a degree of control over the enterprise. This may well have had an appeal in Bath where, by virtue of the incorporation of the city, only the thirty members of the Corporation had the franchise. It enabled the wider charitable elite of the city to become more involved, and to gain a measure of control over the poor rather than leaving them entirely in the hands of parish officers. For members of the medical profession, charitable medical institutions also provided opportunities for the growth of knowledge, for the acquisition of status and for social and financial advancement.

§

The formation of the Casualty Hospital

On November 20th 1787, a small group of men led by the Revd. John Sibley, Rector of Walcot, met to discuss the desirability and feasibility of a hospital to assist those involved in sudden accidents.[10] The group in Bath, including James Norman, a surgeon newly arrived in the city, attributed the need for such an institution to the increase in building work. This had attracted workers to the area, and 'day labourers and poor people' were particularly vulnerable, because of the nature of their work, to the possibility of sudden accidents. The Coroners' Records show that the second biggest cause of accidents after drowning was falling.[11] Men fell off ladders, out of windows, off roofs and into the river, and, while it is difficult to say how many of these accidents were directly work-related, the records show that between 1780 and 1789 there were thirteen accidental deaths recorded, many of which may well have been work-related. Many more accidents will have occurred that resulted in injuries, possibly severe, and possibly leading to permanent disability.

At this early stage, the charity was intended for the parish of Walcot only, and the parish vestry had already agreed to pay five shillings a week for every Walcot parishioner who became a patient in the hospital. The hope was expressed that other Bath parishes would agree to pay a similar amount, thereby making the facility available to their own parishioners. No doubt the parish officers in Walcot saw the sense of supporting a local charity that would have the effect of returning to work as quickly as possible men and women who might otherwise remain a burden on the poor rates. In this way, they were transferring the costs of supporting accident victims and their families from ratepayers, some of whom may have been close to pauperisation, to the more affluent in the parish who, it was hoped, would become subscribers. At the first meeting it was agreed that the Trustees should meet monthly to pass the accounts, and William Anderdon, then still a banker in Bath, was appointed treasurer.[12] Daniel Lysons MD and James Norman, surgeon, had agreed to give their services gratis and their offers were accepted.

It was common practice at the time for charity trustees to supply subscribers with tickets that could then be passed to potential recipients, the number of tickets supplied being related to the size of the donation. In this way it was hoped that only the 'deserving' poor would benefit from the philanthropic generosity of subscribers. Subscribers to the Casualty Hospital, however, were not to be supplied with tickets and, unlike other charities in Bath, accident victims did not need to secure the recommendation of a subscriber before receiving help. The sole criterion for treatment at the hospital was involvement in a severe accident.

January 1788 was a busy month for the Trustees of the new venture: by the third of the month a house at 28 Kingsmead Street had been rented for one year, and by January 10th the first patients had been admitted.[13] In March, the Trustees agreed that the Churchwardens of the other three Bath parishes should be asked to contribute ten guineas to the charity, although they would still be expected to bury their own dead.[14] The problem of burial was one that had been raised at the General Infirmary, since, if the family of the deceased was unable to pay for burial, the expense fell on the parish.[15] The Trustees, therefore, were anxious to avoid any additional expense for the parish that might arise relating to the burial of the very poor.

On Tuesday, March 11th 1788, the Trustees met with the churchwardens and overseers of St. Michael's, St. James's and Abbey parishes to ask for their support.[16] The Abbey churchwardens did not feel able to ask ratepayers to contribute, and Mr. White, a perukemaker who was overseer for St. James's, gave the same reply: only the parishes of St. Michael and Walcot were prepared to support the hospital. On April 1st 1788, the churchwardens of Walcot came to a further agreement with the Trustees. They were prepared to extend their agreement to include not only the parishioners of Walcot, but also anyone residing in Walcot who did not have a settlement either in Walcot, or in any of the other Bath parishes. While Walcot encompassed the 'best' addresses in the city, it also included some of the poorest areas, Avon Street, for example, and the courts and alleys on either side. Here there would have been a concentration of migrant casual labourers, without a settlement in the parish, and the most vulnerable to abject poverty in the event of an accident. Further, Walcot vestry was prepared to pay for anyone who suffered an accident while working in Walcot although not residing there and without a settlement in any other Bath parish. The vestry would also take responsibility for either burial in the event of death, or removal to the parish of settlement in the event of recovery. This was a generous agreement and indicates the high degree of commitment Revd. Sibley and the parish officers had to helping the poor in a parish that was in the thick of the building boom of 1785-1793.[17] As residents of the city, and businessmen, they undoubtedly appreciated the need for migrant workers and the need to keep them, as cheaply as possible, within the city. This provides a good example of a private charity that obtained public funding, something that may have had particular appeal to public administrators, in this case parish overseers, as an oblique method of dealing with the social problem of injury and illness.[18] This also avoided a public admission that the poor had a right to medical care.[19]

On May 20th 1788, Mr. Norman produced his monthly accounts and then left the meeting to attend a patient. Both Dr. Lysons and James Norman were entitled to attend meetings of the Trustees but had no vote. Norman was asked in future to produce accounts in advance of the meeting 'for the better dispatch of business'.[20] This was the first indication that James Norman did not always 'fit in' with the committee. Over the years he was to be reprimanded on a number of occasions for minor infringements of the Rules. Perhaps this is an indication that he was not an ideal committeeman. Nonetheless, after one year at the Casualty Hospital the Trustees awarded him a gratuity of twenty guineas.

§

James Norman

James Norman arrived in Bath in 1783, having trained as a surgeon in Bristol where he had been on the staff of St. Peter's Hospital and the Bristol Royal Infirmary.[21] He had apparently resigned suddenly and without explanation and moved to Bath. He arrived in Bath with his wife, Anne, who was the daughter of Valentine Watkins, esq., of Bristol, and his young son, George.[22] George Norman's entry in Plarr's *Lives of the Fellows of the Royal College of Surgeons* suggests that there was an older son who died in the early nineteenth-century.[23] Munro Smith, the historian of the Bristol Royal Infirmary, described Norman as having 'a rough exterior and a blunt unpolished manner'.[24] Although he was a good practitioner, we can imagine that such a man might not fit well with Bath's medical establishment. There were a number of surgeons in Bath and competition may well have been fierce.

Aligning himself with a new medical charity was a shrewd move and had a number of advantages, both political and financial and in the acquisition of status. For a man with a 'blunt' manner it may not have been easy to break into the Bath medical establishment. At the hospital, Norman was mixing with people such as the Revd. Sibley, rector of the largest parish in the city, covering the most prestigious residential areas as well as the most poverty stricken. Sibley was influential in a number of institutions and well respected. James Norman will also have worked closely with William Anderdon who was treasurer to the charity. Anderdon was a partner in a bank in Bath, and although it went into liquidation in the 1792 crash, he and his family were well respected in the city. William Anderdon was also a member of the Corporation for a number of years and mayor in some of those years, as were other family members. No doubt, through his work at the hospital, Norman would have been able to 'network' with some of the more influential members of the ruling elite in Bath.

Unlike surgeons at the Bath General Hospital, the surgeon at the Casualty Hospital was able to take on apprentices. In November 1792, an advertisement for an apprentice at the Casualty Hospital appeared in *The Bath Chronicle*.[25] Apprenticeship fees were whatever parents of prospective apprentices could be persuaded to pay, so this may well have been a lucrative source of income. There are no details of the premiums paid by apprentices at the Casualty Hospital but, when in 1770, Henry Wright, surgeon, took on William Thomas as an apprentice the premium was £262.[26] The Coroners' Records suggest that student surgeons were working at the Casualty Hospital at least from 1819.[27] Norman's income from the hospital also increased over the years as the charity became more and more successful.

In January 1790, Norman addressed a letter to the Trustees in which he made a number of points concerning surgeons' fees.[28] He claimed that there were no set charges for the work of a surgeon and most were happy to treat the poor for free. For those 'in the middle sphere of life', surgeons were happy to charge fees proportional to their patients' circumstances, although he comments that these fees were rarely adequate. From the rich, surgeons expected 'a more liberal compensation'. Most surgeons charged reasonable amounts but, he claimed, there were a number of his colleagues who 'through avarice' made extortionate demands and were, therefore, a disgrace to their profession. Having given his services free for two years, he felt that it was not unreasonable to ask for a gratuity proportional to the more affluent state of the charity. When it grew even richer, he would expect a greater reward. He wrote that he expected the charity to become more affluent due to the Trustees 'judicial management'. His request was granted and, thereafter, he received a gratuity of forty guineas per annum. This letter reveals James Norman as a man with a commitment to helping the poor, a degree of self-worth, with a strong sense of social justice, and not averse to using flattery to achieve his ends. Throughout the history of the Casualty Hospital, James Norman was adamant that a subscription scheme for funding the hospital should not lead to a system of admittance by ticket, thereby encouraging the continuance of a system of patronage and deference. This insistence on admission on the basis of need only was to prove a major stumbling block to a merger with the Bath City Infirmary and Dispensary.

At the time of writing his letter to the Trustees, James Norman gave his address as St. John's Court, not in the best part of town, and described by R.S. Neale as 'a place of working class settlement'.[29] The Directory for Bath for 1800 lists James Norman as midwife and surgeon, now at 8 New King's Street, a much better address, but still in the south of the city. [30] By 1809 Norman and Son, surgeons, were listed as living at 24 New King's Street.[31] James was sufficiently secure in Bath to have improved his status by changing his address. By now he was sufficiently part of the medical establishment in Bath that in June 1797 there is the first record of him having given medical evidence at a Coroner's Inquest.[32]

§

The work of the Casualty Hospital

The charity flourished and, over the years, the Casualty Hospital increased in size, proving the need for such an institution. The Trustees reported that in their first year they had admitted forty-five patients of whom thirty-seven were discharged well, six died and two remained in the hospital.[33] In January 1792, the Hospital reported that in the years since the Hospital had opened, they had admitted 109 patients, discharged as cured ninety-six, but seven patients had died.[34] The hospital had also treated 600 outpatients. As early as August 1790, two new beds with bed linen and towels were ordered.[35] As well as effecting a cure, it seems likely that, at least for the very poor, being in the Hospital would have involved an improvement in living standards, as patients had a bed, bedclothes, food, drink, care of some sort, and, possibly, emotional or religious comfort.[36]

In January 1791, it was recorded that all ten beds were full and that two more had been ordered, and later in the month the two beds that had been kept for emergency amputations were pressed into general use.[37] Two further beds were added in June, and in November a builder was asked to inspect the garrett with a view to converting it for the use of patients.[38] On May 1st 1792, the Trustees recorded that in the previous years the Hospital had treated 102 in-patients and 690 out-patients.[39] By 1812, it was obvious that the premises in Kingsmead Square were inadequate and James Norman was charged with the job of finding 'a more commodious house'.[40] No progress would appear to have been made as, in September 1819, it was reported that the Hospital had been so full that an apartment had been hired to accommodate patients.[41] It was agreed in January 1820 that the charity would have to either buy or build a new hospital and James Norman was once more given the job of finding suitable premises. He quickly found 4 Pierrepoint Street and was instructed, on January 20th, to buy the premises for £1,000. The sale must have fallen through because he reported on February 1st that he had found a suitable piece of land.[42] The search for new premises, however, came to nothing until the merger with the Bath City Infirmary and Dispensary.

The first approach to the Casualty Hospital by the Bath City Infirmary and Dispensary (then The Pauper Charity) had been made in January 1789. The Casualty Hospital's rejection of the advances of the Pauper Charity had led to the formation of the Bath City Infirmary and Dispensary.[43] In its reply to this early approach, the Casualty Hospital set out its *raison d'etre*. The Hospital was there for 'the reception of casualties without distinction the accident being sufficient recommendation without further enquiry'.[44] The matter was not raised again until late November 1817.[45] There were obvious advantages to a merger: both charities would pay less rent, particularly important as both institutions had a need for larger premises, bills for wages and other expenses would be lower, and the united institution would have, to use a modern phrase, a larger profile in the city. Nevertheless, in 1817, the Casualty Hospital still felt that 'the objections supercede (*sic*) all advantages'.[46]

There were two major areas of disagreement between the two charities - the constitution of the governing body and, probably more importantly, the criteria

fig 1: The United Hospital, Beau Street, c.1849. With the Old Royal Baths in the foreground. Photograph attributed to W. Russell Sedgfield.
Bath in Time – Bath Central Library Collection

for admittance. In the first case, the Casualty Hospital trustees wanted to keep the governing body small and self-perpetuating, while the Infirmary and Dispensary favoured a larger management committee elected by the subscribers. The Casualty Hospital had always taken in-patients solely on the basis of need, whereas the Infirmary and Dispensary preferred to control the intake of patients by means of the recommendatory ticket. The differences indicate an ideological gap between the charities, the Casualty Hospital management being oligarchic, reflecting the Corporation of the city, while, at the same time, appearing more egalitarian through admittance by need alone.

The founding trustees were, in fact, determined to keep a firm and paternalistic check on the charity with as little input from the subscribers as possible except, of course, for their donations. The Infirmary and Dispensary, on the other hand, were prepared to open the management of the charity to subscribers, but wanted to keep control of the intake of patients. Subscribers were able, if they so wished, to play a much more important part in the running of the charity. This reflected more accurately the growing desire among the middling sort for involvement in the management of philanthropy in the country in general, while, at the same time, ensuring that only the 'deserving' poor received help.

After protracted negotiations, a merger was arranged and in the Casualty Hospital minutes a brief entry for February 19th 1823 notes a meeting of subscribers in the Guildhall, chaired by Charles Crook, apothecary and mayor.[47] The Corporation offered a donation of £1,000 towards the erection of a new hospital. It appears that the Corporation had been determined that the two charities should merge and was prepared to use its money to achieve this end.[48] The new institution was called the Bath United Hospital and was the foundation of what Bathonians now know as the Royal United Hospital. **[fig. 1].** It is tempting to speculate that negotiations leading to a merger were delayed by the determination of James Norman to maintain the *status quo* at the Casualty Hospital. As early as April 1820, James Norman inserted a somewhat peevish advertisement in a local paper to the effect that, after thirty years of active service, he was withdrawing as a Trustee because of the proposed merger. He claimed that the Casualty Hospital was abandoning an excellent constitution that had meant the institution had been governed 'in perfect harmony' 'to the entire satisfaction of the Public'. He would, in future, see pregnant women at his own premises.[49] Heavily involved in the merger was James Norman's son, George. Part of the agreement between the two charities was that George Norman was to be appointed surgeon at the new institution.

§

George Norman

George Norman was born around 1783, about the time his parents came to Bath. Nothing is known of his early life or education but it would appear that, after a short spell in London, he became his father's assistant in 1801, and, on June 4th of that year, he became a member of the newly-formed Royal College of Surgeons of England.[50] Plarr's *Lives* suggested that after the death of an elder brother, George began to practice as a surgeon on his own account. Then, in February 1816, George was appointed Assisting Surgeon to his father at the Casualty Hospital and, a month later, James resigned as surgeon and George was appointed in his place. After his resignation, James was appointed as a Trustee and would then have had a full voice on the Committee. Thereafter he was recorded in the minutes as attending regularly as the Hospital Visitor. This was not to visit patients in a social manner but to be available to hear complaints and to check the accounts and twice a year to undertake stocktaking. So, although no longer working in his professional capacity at the hospital, he was still very involved in the running of the charity.

George Norman was married in 1816 to Margaretta, daughter of John Kitson esq., of Bath.[51] Kitson was an apothecary of some note in the city and was Mayor in 1817.[52] George and Margaretta went on to have four daughters, Emma, Louisa, Isabel and Margaretta.

By 1833, James Norman was no longer mentioned in the *Bath Guides* but George was listed as living at No.1 The Circus, one of the most prestigious addresses in the city.[53] Having been elected to the City Corporation in 1812, and, having served his apprenticeship as a councilman, George Norman was made Mayor in 1834. In 1836, when the Municipal Corporations Act was implemented, he was elected as a town councillor for the new Kingsmead ward. He was also made an alderman and a justice of the peace. He was elected Mayor again in 1841, the only mayor to serve both before and after the Municipal Corporations Act. He also became Deputy Lord Lieutenant of the county of Somerset. When he retired from the Bath United Hospital in 1857, he was made one of its Vice-Presidents, and his marble bust was set up in the hall of the hospital.[54] He was presented with a 'testimonial' from 'the working classes' to mark their sense of his services to the public.[55] **[fig.2].**

George Norman died of pleuropneumonia, after a few days illness, on January 17th 1861. He was seventy-eight years old. He had been a much loved and respected presence in the city and his funeral was an occasion for the Corporation and people of Bath to recognise his contribution to the life of the city, particularly to the lives of the poor. The opening lines of a poem written to mark his funeral give a vivid, if somewhat sentimental, view of how George Norman was regarded.

fig 2: **Portrait of George Norman FRCS 1840.** Printed and engraved by W.O. Geller. Published London by Henry Benham Oct. 16th 1840.
Bath in Time – Bath Central Library Collection

'He around him saw a crowd in tears; and said
"Why do you weep?" they answered, "NORMAN's dead!"
"Aye", said, with faltering voice, a loving wife,
"Good Doctor Norman sav'd my husband's life."
"For me," another said, "he did more good,
He cured my ailments and he gave me food."
"I", said another, - "well may I lament;
He sav'd me, fed me, cloth'd me, paid my rent"
Not on poor folks alone did he attend,
The gentry, too, have lost a friend.'

The poem purports to have been written by a stranger to Bath but it gives us some insight, albeit in a rather patronising manner, to the generosity and breadth of George Norman's commitment to helping the poor.[56] The obituary that appeared in *The Lancet*, described George Norman as simple, unaffected, perfectly self-possessed, a strong Liberal and an active politician.[57] At his death he was Consulting Surgeon to the United Hospital, Surgeon to the Puerperal

Charity, Vice-President of the British Medical Association, and Fellow of the Royal Medico-Chirurgical Society.

On the day of George Norman's funeral, the Corporation and other mourners met at the Guildhall, from where they proceeded in twenty carriages up the hill to Bennett Street, where they met members of the medical profession.[58] Norman's family joined the procession at The Circus. In all, forty-one carriages proceeded to the cemetery at Lansdown. Norman's four daughters were in the first carriage but no mention was made of Mrs. Norman. The carriages were followed by a number of mourners on foot although *The Bath Chronicle* stated that, because of some confusion as to the time of the funeral, a number of people intending to attend on foot were too late for the ceremony. This is sadly ironic. The very people who probably owed most to him were unable to pay their last respects by following the procession up the hill to Lansdown. In the south aisle of Bath Abbey, there is a stained glass window by Clayton and Bell entitled 'Christ healing the sick' or 'The cripples' window' after a painting by Frederick Overbeck.[59] It was donated by public subscription in memory of George Norman. [fig.3].

§

The medical profession and charity

Arguably, James and George Norman gained considerably from association with a medical charity, and as part of the management of the Casualty Hospital. There are three areas in particular in which the medical profession had much to gain from voluntary institutions – financial, social, and in an increase of clinical knowledge.[60]

Although many medical men gave of their services free, the contacts they made through charity hospitals may well have led to an increase of patients in their own practices. We know that James Norman eventually gained a steady salary from the Casualty Hospital. Involvement with charities enabled some men to take apprentices for which they could expect a fee. The Royal College of Surgeons' *Lives of the Fellows* claims that George Norman took 'the highest position' as a surgeon in Bath and that his practice 'probably exceeded that of any other provincial surgeon.' For a long period his income was estimated at around £4,000 per annum, and the 1851 Census shows that the Norman

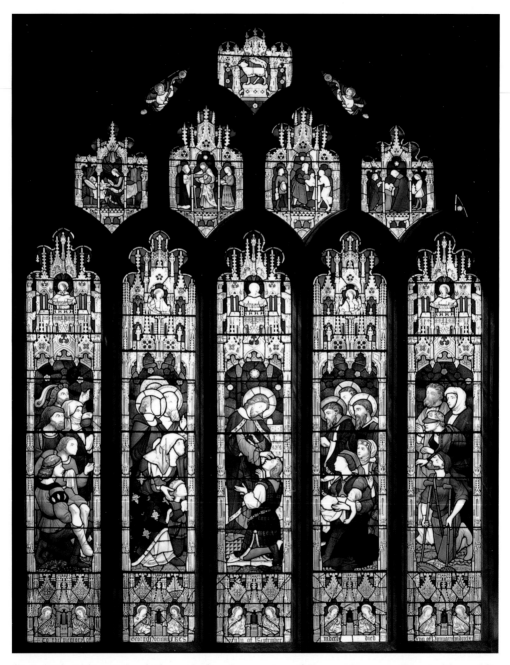

fig 3: Bath Abbey stained glass window in memory of George Norman. Donated by public subscription and designed by Clayton and Bell, this is situated in the south aisle.
Author's collection

household employed seven servants.[61] The acquisition of a 'good' address, wealth, and the ability to teach apprentices would all have resulted in increased status in the local community. Moreover, socially, men stood to gain from their association with other members of the management and, probably more particularly, from association with subscribers. We can trace the rise of James and George Norman through the social strata of Bath from James arriving in Bath as an unknown surgeon in 1788, to George elected Mayor of Bath by 1834, and, at his death, Deputy Lord Lieutenant of the County.

Possibly the greatest area for advancement was in clinical knowledge and the Casualty Hospital provided a locus for education. The Normans used their participation in charity to train the next generation of professionals.[62] They were assisted in this by the great variety of patients they must have encountered presenting with a variety of injuries, illnesses and obstetric problems. It is noticeable from the Coroners' Records that the bodies of most of the patients who died in the Casualty Hospital had autopsies carried out on them. Most of these seem to have taken place after 1819, and this is possibly due to the fact that George Norman took over as surgeon at the hospital in 1817. For example, George Norman conducted an autopsy on the body of James Bapott in July 1819: when, in November 1819, Clement Murphy fell from the back of a carriage and died of his injuries, Frederick Field, George Norman's apprentice, carried out an autopsy: another apprentice, Edwin Skeater, performed an autopsy after Isaac Cox died, and discovered that he had a diseased liver and intestines: it was discovered that Caroline Collins had died of a ruptured liver following a road traffic accident.[63] In addition to his work at the hospital, George Norman frequently assisted Dr. Caleb Hillier Parry with autopsies and surgical experiments. Such experiments were carried out on sheep bred by Parry on his estate on the outskirts of Bath, and frequently took place at 6.30am or 10pm.[64] George Norman contributed a number of papers to professional journals, two of which were on the subject of aneurysm, and one involved a case of full-term extra-uterine foetation, all based on cases from his hospital work. A great deal of anatomical and clinical knowledge will have been gained from these events that would not have otherwise been possible. While the Normans must have gained a good deal from these events, so did the residents of Bath and the wider world, as surgeons became more knowledgeable, more professional and more skilled. The Coroners' Records suggest that the labouring sort in Bath had confidence in the Casualty Hospital and its surgeons.[65]

Conclusion

The formation of a medical charity in Bath, and the development of a Casualty Hospital to treat victims of serious injury, were a direct response by the charitable elite in Bath to the influx of migrant labour to the city to service the building industry, and to the consequent strain on poor law provision in the city parishes. The charity's Trustees were successful in raising funds, treating the injured and gaining the confidence of the labouring poor. The minutes of the Trustees meetings show that the hospital was constantly under pressure for more beds. The need for more space led, eventually, to a merger of the Casualty Hospital with another medical charity in Bath. The two charities would appear to have had somewhat different approaches to medical provision for the poor, and the need to reconcile these ideological differences, delayed the completion of the merger for some years. It may be that the problems between the two charities reflected changing attitudes in the country to philanthropy and the poor.

Involvement with a charity opened up opportunities to James Norman, and later to his son George Norman. Grasping these opportunities enabled father and son to advance both financially and socially, and to gain clinical experience and knowledge. George, in particular, was able to capitalise on his association with the Casualty Hospital. Although their participation in the management of a medical charity in the city benefited James and George Norman, they were not the only beneficiaries. Through George Norman's published work, and through the education of the next generation of practitioners, the inhabitants of Bath benefited as did the wider world.

Notes

1. Barbara Brandon Schnorrenberg, 'Medical Men of Bath', *Studies in Eighteenth Century Culture*, 1984, vol.13, pp.189-203.
2. Ben Wilson, *Decency and Disorder, 1789-1837*, (London, 2007), p.42.
3. Robert Southey, *The Canaan of Physicians, Letters from England, 1803*, cited in *Bath in Quotes*, (Lancaster, 2006), p.100. See also William Congreve, *Orders of his Excellency R____d N____h Esq, 1728*, also cited in *Bath in Quotes*, p.57.
4. Roy Porter, 'Was there a medical enlightenment in eighteenth century England?', *British Journal for Eighteenth Century Studies*, 1982, vol.5, pp.49-63; for quackery in Bath see Roy Porter, *Quacks: Fakers and Charlatans in English Medicine*, (Stroud,

2000), p.140, and Schorrenberg, 'Medical Men', pp.193-195.

5.   *The Bath Chronicle,* December 13th 1798, and June 27th 1799, Bath Central Library.

6.   Tobias Smollett, *The Adventures of Peregrine Pickle,* (London, 1751), chap.70; Christopher Anstey, *The New Bath Guide or Memoirs of the Br-n-r-d Family,* (London, 1766), Letter II, Letter VI.

7.   Schnorrenberg, *Medical Men,* pp.189-193.

8.   Donna T. Andrew, *Philanthropy and Police: London Charity in the Eighteenth Centur,y* (New Jersey, USA, 1989), p.53.

9.   Anne Borsay, *Medicine and Charity in Eighteenth-Century Bath: A Social History of the General Hospital 1739-1830,* (Aldershot,1999); The Casualty Hospital, Bath: Rules and Orders, 1788-1826, (hereafter Rules and Orders), The Wellcome Library for the History and Understanding of Medicine, Manuscript 1094, London.

10.   Rules and Orders.

11.   City of Bath Coroners' Examinations and Inquisitions, 1766-1835, (hereafter Coroners' Records), Bath Record Office.

12.   There were usually five trustees to administer the Casualty Hospital. This is in contrast to the Bath City Infirmary and Dispensary who felt they needed sixteen committee members.

13.   Rules and Orders, January 1788.

14.   Rules and Orders, March 1788.

15.   *The Bath Chronicle,* February 3rd 1780, Bath Central Library.

16.   Rules and Orders, March 1788.

17.   R. S. Neale, *Bath 1680-1850: A Social History or A Valley of Pleasure yet a Sink of Iniquity* (London,1981), Figure 2, p.43.

18.   Jonathan Barry and Colin Jones, *Medicine and Charity before the Welfare State,* (London, 1991), p.3.

19.   Katherine Park has brought to our attention that in Florence doctors were being paid out of public funds to treat the poor as early as the thirteenth century. Katherine Park, 'Healing the poor: hospitals and medical assistance in renaissance Florence', in Barry and Jones, *Medicine and Charity before the Welfare State,* pp.26-46, p.29. The joint poorhouse committee for Abbey and St. James appointed a surgeon to attend the poor in both parishes on May 6th 1784; on August 17th 1790 Mr. Nick Kelly was appointed to undertake all surgery and midwifery at the poorhouse. Poorhouse Committee Book – St. Peter and St. Paul and St. James, Bath Record Office.

20.   Rules and Order, May 20th 1788.

21.   John Kirkup, 'A pioneer accident service: Bath Casualty Hospital, 1788-1826', in Roger Rolls, Jean Guy and John Richard Guy, (eds) *A Pox on the Provinces:*

Proceedings of the 12th Congress of the British Society for the History of Medicine, (Bath, 1990), p. 50-58.

22. *County Families (Walford's County Families) of the United Kingdom,* British Library, (1860), quoted in a letter from the Somerset County Archivist to Mr. A. K. Wallis, Clippings File, Bath Central Library.

23. Plarr's *Lives of the Fellows, Royal College of Surgeons,* Clippings File, Bath Central Library.

24. Quoted in Kirkup, 'A pioneer accident service.'

25. *The Bath Chronicle,* November 8th, 1792, Bath Central Library.

26. Jan Chivers, 'A Resonating Void': Strategies and Responses to Poverty, Bath, 1770-1835' (unpublished PhD Thesis, Bath Spa University, 2006), p.106 and n.25, p.134.

27. Coroners' Records. On April 6th 1819 Michael Symons, described as assistant to George Norman, gave evidence at the inquest on the body of Benjamin Foreman. On three occasions between October 1819 and April 2nd 1821 Frederick Field, also described as assistant to George Norman, gave medical evidence at inquests. On two of those occasions the deceased had died at the Casualty Hospital. This suggests that George Norman was taking students at the Casualty Hospital before the merger.

28. Rules and Orders, January, 1790.

29. Neale, *Bath a Social History,* p.217.

30. *The Directory for Bath,* 1800, Bath Central Library.

31. *The Directory for Bath,* 1809, Bath Central Library.

32. Coroners' Records, June 12th 1797.

33. *The Bath Chronicle,* January 15th 1789.

34. *The Bath Chronicle*, January 5th 1792.

35. Rules and Orders, August 1790.

36. Rules and Orders, August 1790, 2 new bedsteads were ordered with 2 sets of sheets, 2 sets of blankets, 2 covers, 2 shifts and 6 towels. On July 5th 1791 linen was bought to make 12 towels, 6 pillowcases and 4 pairs of sheets. On July 3rd 1792 it was reported that the management had bought 2 Bibles, 12 Books of Common Prayer and 24 copies of Bishop Gibsons' *Serious Advice to Persons who have been Sick,* the latter to be given to every patient.

37. Rules and Orders, January 1791.

38. Rules and Orders, November 1791.

39. Rules and Orders, May 1792

40. Rules and Orders, 1812.

41. Rules and Orders, September 1819.

42. Rules and Orders, January and February 1820.

43. Rules and Orders, January 1792.

44. Rules and Orders, May 1792.

45. Rules and Orders, November 1817.

46. Rules and Orders, November 1817.

47. Rules and Orders, February 1823.

48. There is no indication in the Minutes as to why this should have happened.

49. This advertisement appeared on 12 April 1820, probably in *The Bath and Cheltenham Gazette*. It is untitled but can be seen in The Hunt Collection, vol.1, p.284, Bath Central Library.

50. Plarr's *Lives of the Fellows of the Royal College of Surgeons*; www.rcseng.ac.uk, accessed May 7th 2008.

51. Letter from the Somerset County Archivist to Mr A. K. Wallis, Clippings File, Bath Central Library.

52. Warren Derry, Notes on various visitors to, and inhabitants of, Bath, (unpublished manuscript, 1975), Bath Central Library.

53. *The Bath Guide*, 1833, Bath Central Library.

54. Royal College of Surgeons of England, www.rcseng.ac.uk, accessed April 10th 2008. Source: *Lancet*, 1861, i, 127.

55. *The Bath Chronicle*, January 24th 1861.

56. *The Stranger in Bath on the memorable funeral of Jan. 25, 1861*, was written by Charles Empson of 7, Terrace Walk, Bath, Hunt Pamphlets, Vol.3, Bath Central Library.

57. Royal College of Surgeons of England, www.rcseng.ac.uk, accessed 10 April 2008. Source: *Lancet*, 1861, i, 127.

58. *Bath Chronicle*, January 31st 1861.

59. Hazel Symons, *Bath Abbey Stained Glass Windows*, (Bath, undated).

60. Anne Borsay, *Medicine and Charity*, p.115.

61. Royal College of Surgeons of England, www.rcseng.ac.uk, accessed April 10th 2008. Source: *Lancet*, 1861, i, 127.

62. Frederick Field, an apprentice to George Norman at the Casualty Hospital, went on to become the first Medical Officer at the new workhouse built as a consequence of the Poor Law Amendment Act of 1834.

63. Coroners' Records, James Bapott, July 10th 1819; Clement Murphy, November 12th 1819; Isaac Cox, July 13th 1828; Caroline Collins, September 12th, 1831.

64. Sholem Glaser, *The Spirit of Enquiry, Caleb Hillier Parry, MD, FRS*, (Stroud, 1995), p.35.

65. Coroners' Records, John David, July 21st 1808; Charles Lacey, September 20th 1809; Harriet Carnell, February 25th 1820.

The truly benevolent Lady Isabella King, 1772-1845

Jackie Collier

In 1809 *The Improved Bath Guide* proudly called attention to 'the benignity of disposition which characterises the people of this highly favoured city.'[1]Amongst the burgeoning numbers involved in the foundation and support of Bath's wealth of new charities was Lady Isabella King (1772-1845), a single Irish gentlewoman from Boyle in the County of Roscommon in the west of Ireland. Her innovative and radical ideas, implemented amid a new, more structured and discriminate philanthropic environment, were devised to address specific contemporary social problems. These ideas were put into practice first with the Monmouth Street Society in 1805,[2] and subsequently, in 1816, with the Ladies Association, and demonstrated not only her strength and determination to succeed but also highlighted women's growing power and autonomy, in a still male-led arena, and established her as an extraordinary woman in the field at the time.

§

Early Family Life

Lady Isabella Letitia King or 'Bell' as she was affectionately named by her father shortly after her birth,[3] was born in October 1772 at 15 Henrietta Street, Dublin. **[fig.1]**. Her father was Edward, 1st earl of Kingston and her mother, who died when Lady Isabella was just twelve years old, was Jane Caulfield, the illegitimate daughter but heiress of Thomas Caulfield of Donamon Castle Co. Roscommon. **[fig.2]**. Proclaimed the beauty of the family by her father, Lady Isabella had three sisters, Jane and Eleanor, seventeen and fourteen years her elder respectively and a younger sister Frances. She also had three brothers, Henry and William who both died before reaching adulthood and Robert, Viscount Kingsborough who was eighteen years her senior and who would later inherit the title of 2nd earl of Kingston.

Facing: fig 1: Portrait of Lady Isabella King.
Patroness of the Monmouth Street Society and
creator of the Ladies Association.
Bath in Time – Bath Central Library Collection

fig 2: Edward, 1st Earl of Kingston. (1726-1797) by Hussey
Courtesy of Anthoney King-Harman & King House Collection, Boyle, Co. Roscommon, Ireland

Family life for Isabella revolved around the family homes of Kingston Lodge on the Rockingham estate near Boyle in County Roscommon **[fig.3]** and the family's town house at Henrietta Street in Dublin. It is also likely that she spent time at Mitchelstown Castle, the home of her brother Robert and his wife

Caroline and their children who, by dint of the age difference, were Lady Isabella's contemporaries. While in their company it is possible that she met Mary Wollstonecraft, radical thinker and controversial campaigner for women's educational equality, who, employed as a tutor to Robert and Caroline's eldest daughters, Margaret and Mary, would profoundly influence their beliefs and affect their future lives.[4]

As an elite member of Irish society Lady Isabella would have also experienced life in fashionable society. Dublin was an exciting capital and entertainments for the wealthy were lavish. The fashionable visited the theatres and listened to concerts, attended masquerades, card parties and balls in the assembly rooms. The King family were an integral part of this social scene and mixed with Dublin's leading citizens. Indeed, Lady Isabella's sister, Eleanor, or Nelly as she was better known by family members, wrote in her diary that she much preferred the Dublin life of parties and balls to days of fishing and dining at home on the Kingston estate in Boyle. However life in the country was not all doom and gloom. The happy atmosphere which accompanied life at Kingston Lodge was recorded by Isabella's close friend, Elizabeth Smith, when she made several visits to Kingston Lodge between 1796 and 1797. In a letter to Isabella she recalled 'the three happy weeks at the hospitable mansion of Lord Kingston'.[5]

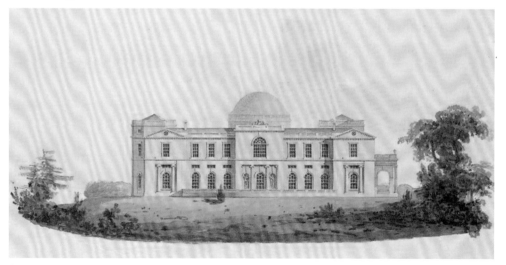

fig 3: Rockingham House. Designed by John Nash and drawn by Repton. Isabella's family home, Kingston Lodge, was situated in the grounds of Rockingham.
Courtesy of Lady Joan Dunn & King House Collection, Boyle, Co. Roscommon, Ireland

It was also part of the Irish aristocratic social calendar to visit the English spas in the season. Writer Richard Lovell Edgeworth mocked this annual outing as a refuge from their luxurious living at home and commented that they flocked to such places like birds of passage. Many visited Bath and the arrivals column in *The Bath Chronicle* lists many members of the King family, who visited the city from the mid-eighteenth century, including Lady Isabella's father, brother Robert and her two elder sisters.

Destined for more than a life as a spinster aunt, Isabella left Ireland for Bath somewhere between 1798 and 1802.[6] It is not clear why she moved to Bath but a letter written by Elizabeth Smith may provide a clue. Concerned for the safety of the King family in the midst of the uncertainties caused by the French Revolution, Elizabeth was convinced they should leave Ireland. 'Amidst all our fears on the subject of the French invasion we could not help encouraging some faint hope that Bath might be thought a safer place than Ireland for the Kingston family'.[7] By 1802 and aged 30, Lady Isabella had taken up permanent residence in Bath and was living at 7 Great Bedford Street, a new and fashionable area just behind the Royal Crescent. Joining the social circles of the city's elite residents and visitors, she had begun to participate in Bath's growing charitable network, part of the increasingly important and changing charitable arena of early- nineteenth century England.

§

Charity in early nineteenth-century England

In a progressively urban society philanthropy had experienced a subtle shift in the eighteenth century. Traditional patterns of charitable activity, focussed on individual benefaction, often unregulated and typically characterised by endowed charities and trusts, was in part replaced by a collective more organised and discriminate model of giving, dedicated to alleviating specific contemporary social problems. Its character was exemplified in the diverse array of specialised voluntary societies, created by the beginning of the nineteenth century to address these problems and which acted as controlling intermediaries between individual philanthropists and the needy. Such new charities sought out and rewarded only those genuinely in need. Sir James Stephen proclaimed: 'ours is an age of societies…for the cure of every sorrow by which our land or our race can be visited'.[8]

Within this picture there emerged a new role for women. Legitimised by their role as moral guardians within the home, philanthropy was seen as an accepted arena of activity outside. Qualities of compassion, tenderness and sensitivity, applied to the needs of the dependent and afflicted, were perceived as feminine virtues and were encouraged to a degree but men held all the positions of power.[9] With limited opportunity and little freedom of action in a still dominantly patriarchal society, women tended to be cast in the subordinate role of helpers, involved in the practical day-to-day maintenance and support of male-run, charitable institutions. A few however, either unhappy or frustrated with the restricted role allotted to them or with the passion and desire to improve the situation of those in need, embraced a more active role. They were bold enough to cross the boundaries set for their sex to become sources of organisational strength at a local level,[10] establishing their own charities, generally female focused, where they exercised direct responsibility. Lady Isabella was one such person and Bath's charitable arena was an ideal location.

§

Bath and Charity

As the leading leisure resort in the country, Bath was certainly not typical of an English town at the time. Its steady stream of short-term visitors from the affluent and leisured classes, coupled with an ever growing resident elite population, provided an unusually high proportion of potential givers. At the same time Bath also attracted the poor who came to seek employment which, by the nature of the city, tended to be seasonal. Irregular employment meant irregular income which, coupled with the unstable economic climate at the time, created financial hardship among the labouring classes. At the same time Bath also attracted large numbers of beggars and vagrants who came to take advantage of the wealthy.

The complex demographic nature of the city demanded a charitable network which identified and supported the impoverished and, as the eighteenth century progressed and the numbers of needy increased, so the nature and numbers of charities in the city developed accordingly. By the beginning of the nineteenth century, Bath hosted a diverse array of charitable institutions which were tailored specifically to the needs of its inhabitants and which rivalled the growth and diversity of benevolence nationwide. The atmosphere of charitable benevolence in the city is reported in Meyler's 1820 edition of *The Bath Guide*. It affirms that 'in no place is the hand of true benevolence more liberally employed than in the city; nor can any place boast of more excellent charitable institutions than are established in Bath and generally supported by voluntary subscriptions of the residents and visitors'.[11]

Historians suggest that by the beginning of the nineteenth century Bath had slowly evolved from a stylish resort for elite fashionable groups into a popular residential location and although the city still received large numbers of visitors their social range widened. With so many arrivals and residents it was no longer a select enclave for the aristocracy and gentry who up until mid-century had been its defining visitors and the nature of social participation altered. Private gatherings and 'at homes' amongst the titled and wealthier residents and visitors increased and created cliques and private circles in an erstwhile open society. Katherine Plymley, a regular visitor to the spa between 1794 and 1807, observed and commented on the continued participation at public social gatherings yet her journals are full of accounts of numerous private parties to which she was invited and attended.[12] These private networks of likeminded people fostered the new and growing charitable ethos in the city. Visiting Bath in 1810, Lord Glenverbie commented on one particular group: 'There is a set of bluestocking ladies here….Lady Isabella King is I understand at the head of this Areopagus',[13] and looking back in 1852, George Monkland confirmed the intellectual 'salons of Lady Isabella King'.[14]

§

Lady Isabella, the philanthropist

Indeed the conception of the Monmouth Street Society can be attributed to one such gathering. At an evening party held by Lady Isabella at her home on January 6th 1805, a discussion arose as to what could be done best for the benefit of Bath. Prominent local figure, John Shute Duncan, suggested that one of the greatest nuisances was the swarm of street beggars who came down from London and other parts to impose on the charitable in Bath.[15] Resolved to do something, Isabella and her guests were determined not only to preserve a reliable public environment by ridding the streets of beggars. They also wanted to provide assistance to those in real need. The question was how? Their idea sought to replace the giving of money to those on the streets, with a relief ticket system whereby the claims of beggars could be investigated, and instances of genuine distress identified and relieved. The principle for this scheme, which clearly embraced the new ideology of the 'deserving poor', expressed a message which would be repeated again and again by similar charitable organisations throughout the century. It said 'alms given in the street, without investigation are bounties on idleness and fraud,...every shilling so received is a robbery from real distress'.[16] At the time these were novel investigative techniques, untried anywhere else, and reveal a concern by those who devised them to re-educate not only the seeker of alms but also the potential charitable donor.

Lady Isabella took a leading role as its first patroness and as host to the charity's early meetings. The Monmouth Street Society was a forerunner of similar institutions later founded in London, Edinburgh, Oxford and Colchester. Her involvement demonstrates a propensity to address, with other leading, male philanthropists in Bath, contemporary social problems in pioneering ways and established her reputation as a leading player in Bath's charitable hierarchy. Indeed her work was thus acknowledged by the Society's committee. On the title page of their annual report for many years it stated 'this society is greatly indebted for its foundation and advancement to the zeal and exertions of Lady Isabella King'[17] and a miniature of her which was presented to the society in 1860, hung in the committee room until the Society's offices were destroyed in the Second World War.

§

The Ladies Association

However it was Lady Isabella's creation of The Ladies Association, her most ambitious and personal project, which truly demonstrated her tenacity and initiative. By 1813, in her forties, Lady Isabella turned her thoughts to the formation of this institution, an innovative and radical undertaking which would occupy her mind and time for much of the remainder of her life.

Its conception can be dated back to a letter written to her sister. In it she wrote of a 'plan' still 'vague and undefined' which aimed to provide assistance in the form of a conventual home for gentlewomen who were, by the death of their parents, 'left with no fortune or income and much reduced below the state of comfort to which they have been accustomed.'[18] Lady Isabella believed these women were often forced into prostitution in order to survive. Her plan involved the establishment of a community 'so regulated as to possess the advantage of a convent without its vows or unnecessary restrictions'.[19] which would consist of Lady Renters who were single women of independent fortune, similar to Isabella herself, with no ties, who, by paying for comfortable accommodation 'reduce[d] the payments of the remainder to a convenient limit without subjecting them to any unpleasant feeling of pecuniary obligation.'[20] The remainder, whom Isabella called Associates, were single or widowed women in reduced circumstances, possessing insufficient income to rent apartments. They were expected to pay an annual sum of fifty pounds for board which would entitle them to a small furnished bedroom.

Describing herself as 'a gentlewoman of some fortune',[21] Lady Isabella's annual income amounted to six hundred pounds a year, enough to support herself but insufficient to fund a charitable venture such as The Ladies Association. Reminiscing later, she commented 'had any individual stepped forward, able and willing to form the establishment, no committee would have been necessary as the rules and regulations and every necessary arrangement would have depended on the wishes of the founder'.[22] Her noble status provided her with the platform from which to act. Nevertheless, even those who moved in the highest circles, and who were anxious for such institutions to succeed did not have the drive and determination displayed by Lady Isabella.[23] She revealed the depth of her passion in her acknowledgement of the enormity of the task whilst remaining constant in her belief in the cause. In her letter to Jane she commented: 'if the object in view be indeed as good as my imagination pictures it, and if the evils which it is intended to lessen be as real as I believe them to be, the thing is worth any effort which can be made.'[24] Friend and supporter Mary Fairfax, attested to this image of Lady Isabella declaring: 'I feel the business is in the hands of one whose head and heart are equal to and wholly devoted to the object.'[25]

Although Isabella's vision embraced the foundation of institutions throughout England and Ireland, doubts as to the feasibility of such a venture and her own insecurities surrounding her ability to organise such an undertaking, shaped her decision to form a primary, experimental

fig 4: Bailbrook House, near Bath c.1830. A later view of Isabella's primary, experimental establishment, opened in June 1816.
Bath in Time – Bath Central Library Collection

establishment which was opened at Bailbrook House, near Bath in June 1816. **[fig.4]**. Indeed even its most ardent supporters expressed their doubts as to its practicability, recognising the many problems associated with a 'very new plan'. The experimental institution at Bailbrook sought 'to ascertain whether under good regulations [and with] ladies of virtue and respectability, the differences which have been brought forward may be removed.'[26] As there were no similar institutions on which The Ladies Association could model itself, many letters written to and from Lady Isabella reveal the difficulties in establishing rules and regulations that a communal institution would demand. The Bishop of St. David's voiced concerns for the preservation of harmony in a community where no one individual possessed authority to prevent 'the selfish from encroaching on the comforts of those more disinterested.'[27] Four years later the problem had still not been resolved. Local supporter and monk

Peter Baines, empathised: 'most sincerely do I wish your Ladyship may discover some principle which may bind together your infant community.'[28] Even as late as 1830 physician Ogilvie Porter still pondered 'how persons so congregated should be governed.'[29]

As crucial was the selection of inmates. Lady Isabella took the advice of Reginald Heber, Bishop of Calcutta, who believed personal 'merit the only recommendation which can ensure admittance and placing the power to select inmates in the hands of those <u>only who are to reside with the persons they</u> nominate.'[30] Fears for the intentions of some potential inmates provide an insight into the possible dangers and problems which were encountered in this process. Writing to prospective applicants, Lady Isabella communicated her concerns that some may view the institution as 'a transient resting place...or lodging house.'[31] Perhaps her greatest anxiety was that it should be seen as 'an introduction into Bath society and a desirable abode for young ladies who are speculating on their advancement in life.'[32]

> The undertaking was criticised by many. There was a general belief that a society of <u>Women-English Women</u> belonging to the Church of <u>England</u> could never be expected to live together in peace- that their love of variety and change, their impatience of restraint, and above all the absence of any religious bond would render it impossible to give it stability or happiness to such an association and that therefore endowments for such establishments would be useless.[33]

Scepticism and reticence to support ideas for such institutions had abounded throughout the eighteenth century, so it was probably no coincidence that an experiment such as this had never before been attempted. Isabella stoically bore discourteous treatment from many, including extreme impertinence from the 'Bath Gossips'.[34]

Although her disappointment is evident in the tone of her letters which relate to these criticisms and public objection clearly limited her aspirations, she was determined to try to make a success of her venture. Once embarked on the task however, she realised her own limitations. She revealed the fears and insecurities that perhaps any woman in her position would have felt when undertaking such a venture in a male-dominated society.

When I reflect on my own want of talent to give it arranged practical form, my inability to carry it into effect and the difficulty of influencing those persons in power whose aid is necessary to give it consequence and respectability, I feel astonished at myself for indulging on such sanguine hopes of it being realised.[35]

Nevertheless, from the outset The Ladies Association commanded an impressive list of supporters. A network of both men and women including family members, influential national figures and local people assumed a variety of roles in the undertaking. The society was honoured by the sanction of Queen Charlotte who visited Lady Isabella at Bailbrook House in 1817. *The Bath Chronicle* reported that the visiting party was 'highly gratified with their visit to this association of ladies' which the Queen called 'a blessed asylum'.[36] Patrons and patronesses to the institution included eight high-ranking noblewomen and four Bishops, and a prominent evangelical presence reflected Lady Isabella's own religious views. Hannah More, a regular visitor to Bath, supported the undertaking, guardians of the society included William Wilberforce and Thomas Babington, and in September 1829 the institute was noticed in the evangelical journal *The Christian Observer*.

But Isabella was the powerhouse of the organisation, making important decisions independently and on a daily basis. In a letter written to her by Sir Benjamin Hobhouse, her financial adviser, regarding the possible purchase of Bailbrook House in 1821, he confirmed her as an astute and able player. 'That your Ladyship will not proceed without due caution and circumspection, but carefully look into all the outgoings of every kind as well as into every other point, I am quite certain.'[37] Lady Isabella was the central force surrounding both the creation and management of the Ladies Association, acting as both patroness and president and ultimately living at both Bailbrook and Cornwallis House. Her dedication to the institution which she called 'this child of my own brain' was total.[38]

The sale of Bailbrook House in 1821 enforced a move to Cornwallis House in Clifton, Bristol. Although initially the institution flourished there, Isabella felt alienated from her friends and the philanthropic support network in Bath which was so important to her. With her strength and spirits worn down by the continued exertion of body and mind required after the loss of Bailbrook, a place in which she had fondly hoped to see the Institution permanently established, she wrote of it and Bath:

> Its vicinity to Bath had placed her within reach of cordial friends and advisers. In every difficulty she could have recourse to friends and talented neighbours who had leisure and inclinations to assist her. All who know Bath honour how distinguished it has been for social and benevolent feeling and after bathing in its sunshine for so many years the transition to Clifton chilled and almost paralysed all the powers of her mind.[39]

By 1833, dwindling numbers of residents saw the Society in decline. Isabella attributed its failure to a lack of internal cohesion amongst residents and a lack of support from friends and others of her class. With her health, strength and spirits failing and feeling evermore harassed and anxious by the demanding responsibilities of the institution which had almost exclusively occupied her attention for seventeen years, she made the decision to withdraw, but admitted that it was the place in which she had hoped to end her days.

With no successor willing to step forward, Cornwallis House was sold in 1838 and, consistent with Isabella's wishes the funds were devoted to religious and charitable endeavours. But she refused to give up hope that the institution would be re-established. Of the poet Robert Southey, a zealous supporter who called her the 'Clara or Teresa of Protestant England labouring for the benefit of her sex',[40] she said, 'I should be sorry if he were to think I had given up the institution in <u>despondency as to its usefulness</u>', continuing, 'it is my intention to write to him fully….to state the opinions which my sixteen years experience have taught me to form, if in his hands, might be made of some little use to any other lady willing to engage in the task of forming a similar institution or re establishing that which was already begun.'[41]

§

Conclusion

Lady Isabella's philanthropic endeavours have until now remained unrecognised and the impact she had on the shape of women's experience has only recently begun to be evaluated. There is no doubt, however, of her strength of character, her belief in her cause, with both The Monmouth Street Society and The Ladies Association. Her preparedness to adopt more direct responsibility by challenging conventional ideals regarding women's role in the philanthropic arena witnessed by all who knew her, establish her as an extraordinary woman. Yet at the time it seems that her reputation only extended as far as her friends who acknowledged her 'indefatiguable zeal'[42] and her 'devotion of herself to purposes of the most important kind'[43] and those who knew her locally. Praised in Bath for her charitable contribution, she was proclaimed 'the truly benevolent Lady Isabella King'.[44]

Notes

1. *Improved Bath Guide,* (Wood & Co., 1809), p.52.
2. The Monmouth Street Society was initially called The Bath Society for the Suppression of vagrants, Street Beggars and Impostors, Relief of Occasional Distress and Encouragement of Industry but was renamed in 1851.
3. King Harman papers, D/4168/A/5/21, April 18th 1773, Public Record Office Northern Ireland.
4. With no direct evidence to confirm or deny any connection between Wollstonecraft and Lady Isabella it is impossible to determine whether her actions in the philanthropic arena were influenced by Wollstonecraft. It is certain however that Wollstonecraft made a strong impression on the minds of Lady Isabella's two cousins, Margaret and Mary. Later in life both girls were involved in events which would bring scandal and disrepute to their family. In 1797 Mary eloped to London with Caroline's half brother Colonel Henry Fitzgerald. Mary was recovered by her parents but a confrontation between Mary's father and brother with Henry resulted in Henry's death. Both were tried for his murder but were found not guilty. Mary's elder sister, Margaret, who was Wollstonecraft's favourite, entered into what would be an unhappy marriage with the earl of Mountcashell when she was just 19. Some years later Margaret admitted that she was 'guilty of numerous errors and none greater than that of marrying at the age of 19 a man whose character was perfectly opposite hers'. While on a visit to Italy in 1804, she met and fell in love with Irish lawyer George Tighe and the following year she left her husband, her children, some of whom she would never see again and Ireland for Tighe and Italy. Margaret and Mountcashel were later divorced. Later in life Margaret wrote 'almost the only person of superior merit with whom I had been intimate in my early days was an enthusiastic

female who was my governess from 14 to 15 years old, for whom I felt unbounded admiration because her mind appeared more noble and understanding, more cultivated than any other I had known, from the time she left me my chief objects were to correct those faults she had pointed out and to cultivate my understanding of as much as possible.'

5. Harriet Bowdler (ed.), *Letters in Prose and Verse by Miss Elizabeth Smith lately died,* (T. Cadell, 1824), p.61.

6. Writing to Lady Isabella in September 1798, Elizabeth revealed a determination that her friend should 'seek for happiness in rational employments' for which she believed Lady Isabella 'was more suited.' She continued 'one can allow those to spend their lives in folly, whose minds are incapable of anything better, but such as yours *should* not be thrown away as I am persuaded it *will* not'. Bowdler, *Letters in Prose and Verse,* p.110.

7. Bowdler, *Letters in Prose and Verse,* p.65.

8. Sir James Stephen, *Essays in Ecclesiastical Biography,* (Longman & Co., 1860), 4th edn. p.581.

9. Catherine Hall, *White, Male and Middle Class. Exploration in Feminism and History,* (Polity, 1992), p.102.

10. Mary Ryan, 'The Power of Women's Networks', J.L. Newton et al, *Sex and Class and Women's History,* (Routledge &Keegan Paul, 1995), p.169.

11. *The Original Bath Guide,* (Meyler &Son, 1820).

12. Diaries of Katherine Plymley, 1791-1827, Shropshire Record Office, cited in Ellen Wilson, 'A Shropshire Lady in Bath, 1794-1807', *Bath History Vol IV* (Millstream Books, 1992), pp.95-123.

13. Sylvester Douglas, *The Diaries of Sylvester Douglas (Lord Glenverbie),* (Constable, 1928), pp.52-3.

14. G. Monkland, *The Literature and Literati of Bath, 'An essay read at the Literary Club,* (R. E. Peach, 1854), p.44.

15. Percy Vere Turner, *Charity for a Hundred Years. History of the Monmouth Street Society, 1805 to 1904,* (G. Godwin, c.1914), p.2.

16. Bath Society for the Suppression of Vagrants: report for 1809, (Richard Crutwell,1810), pp.3-5, cited in M.J.D. Roberts, 'Reshaping the Gift Relationship', *International Review of Social History, Vol.3,* 1991, pp.201-231.

17. Turner, *Charity for a Hundred Years,* p.77.

18. General and Household Correspondence of Lady Isabella King, Doncaster archives, DD/DC/H7/13.

19. DD/DC/H7/13, letter to Lady Isabella's sister, Jane, 1813.

20. DD/DC/H7/9, printed prospectus, March 1827.

21. DD/DC/H7/13 letter to Jane, 1813.

22. DD/DC/H7/16, letter to Dowager Countess Manvers, Jan. 1819.
23. Writing to Lady Isabella in 1813, Mrs. Iremonger identified two such high-ranking women. 'It is not many years ago since the Dowager Lady Spencer was very earnest for such a foundation and scheme as you propose and would be very likely to take an active part on such an occasion….When you next see Mrs—- pray ask her whether our Queen had not a similar idea in contemplation formerly.' Indeed Fanny Burney's diary reveals that Queen Charlotte herself was a member of a similar institution in Germany before her marriage. 'We have protestant nunneries in Germany. I belonged to one which was under the Imperial protection….These nunneries are intended for young ladies of little fortunes and high birth….I had the Cross and Order, but believe I gave it away when I came to England.' *Diary and Letters of Madame D'Arblay Vol II 1781-1786*, ed. Charlotte Barrett, (Henry Colburn, 1854), p.341-342, DD/DC/H7/15, Nov. 26th 1813.
24. DD/DC/H7/13, letter to Jane, 1813.
25. DD/DC/H7/15, letter to Lady Isabella from Mary Fairfax, May 18th 1814.
26. DD/DC/H7/16, letter to Miss F, 1818.
27. DD/DC/H7/15, letter from the bishop of St. David's, Feb. 18th 1817.
28. DD/DC/H7/16, letter from Peter Baines, Dec. 21st 1816.
29. DD/DC/H7/3, letter from O. Porter, Jan. 1st 1830.
30. DD/DC/H7/16, letter to Dowager Countess Manvers, Jan. 1819.
31. DD/DC/H7/16, letter to Miss F, 1818.
32. DD/DC/H7/15, letter to Hon Miss Wodehouse, Feb. 4th 1817.
33. DD/DC/H7/16, letter to Miss F, 1818.
34. DD/DC/H7/15, letter to Lady Willoughby, Oct. 10th 1816.
35. DD/DC/H7/13, letter re plan.
36. *The Bath Chronicle,* Dec. 3rd 1817.
37. DD/DC/H7/6, letter from Sir Benjamin Hobhouse, 1821.
38. DD/DC/H7/15, letter to Lady Wilton, 1813.
39. DD/DC/H7/1/9, notes, 1829.
40. Robert Southey, *Sir Thomas More: Or Colloquies on the Progress and Prospects of Society,* Vol II (John Murray, 1829), p.305.
41. DD/DC/H7/15, letter to the Bishop of Salisbury, June 27th 1833.
42. DD/DC/H7/15, letter from Lady Carysfort, June 22nd 1816.
43. DD/DC/H7/15, letter from Mrs Iremonger, Nov. 26th 1813.
44. *The New Bath Guides,* 1813-1820.

ADMIT

TO THE PERFORMANCE

AT

Assembly Rooms, Bath

On Monday the 10th Nov. 1851.

THE CURTAIN RISES AT *½ past 7* O'CLOCK PRECISELY.

(Signed) W.H. Wills Hony

PAID

Charles Dickens and the Guild of Literature and Art Ticket, 1851

Anne Buchanan

This ticket is part of a small group of items in Bath Library's collection of ephemeral material. The ticket – about 20 x 16½ cm – was for entry to a performance by the Guild of Literature and Art at the Assembly Rooms on Monday November 10th 1851. The artwork was commissioned from E .C. Ward by Charles Dickens, and shows artist Richard Wilson entering a pawn shop, and author Daniel Defoe leaving the bookseller Edmund Curll with a rejected manuscript. The Guild was formed in 1850 by Dickens and writer Edward Bulwer Lytton to raise money to help struggling authors and artists through fundraising events. The 1851 performances were of Bulwer Lytton's marathon five-act farce *Not so bad as we seem* and a comedy *Mr Nightingale's Diary* by Dickens and Mark Lemon, editor of *Punch*. The majority of the cast were enthusiastic amateur actors, such as John Tenniel the cartoonist, author Wilkie Collins as well as Dickens and Lemon. Bulwer Lytton's play received a Royal premier in May at Devonshire House in London in front of Queen Victoria and Prince Albert, after which there were plans to take the play on tour, starting with Bath and Bristol in November 1851. [fig. 1].

The Bath performance appears to mark the end of Dickens' close relationship with Bath. Since he was a young reporter visiting Bath in 1835 he had used the city and its citizens as inspiration, yet after this performance Dickens returned to the city only twice – in 1867 and 1869 for public readings. It has been suggested that, because of the poor reception of this performance, Dickens never forgave Bath,[1] and thus did not return until encouraged to by his publishers. The reviews in *The Bath Chronicle*[2] read as if the critic wearied of the performance – which did not end until 1am – as he comments that the 'dialogue is not sparkling', but the actors transformed the 'dull comedy' into a 'delightful entertainment'. The audience took time to warm to Lytton's play, but it 'grew loud and enthusiastic at the end', and they were later kept in a 'roar' by the second comedy. The critic apparently did not think much of the text of the play, nor some of the performances, although he did single out Dickens' efforts as

Facing: Detail from entry ticket, Nov. 10 1851.
To the Performance at the Assembly Rooms, Bath.
The curtain rises at half past seven o'clock precisely.
Bath in Time – Bath Central Library Collection

fig 1: Entry ticket to Dickens performance of Not so Bad as we Seem, Nov. 10 1851. Charles Dickens and his companions performed this play by Sir Edward Bulwer Lytton, followed by his own farce, Mr Nightingale's Diary, in which he took six different parts.
Bath in Time – Bath Central Library Collection

fig 2: Portrait of Charles Dickens, 1867. Engraved from a photograph by J. Gurney & Son
Bath in Time – Bath Central Library Collection

amongst the best. The audience eventually reacted enthusiastically by their standards, although this seems not to have been apparent to Dickens, who describes them as a 'dull audience', particularly in comparison to the Bristol audience whose 'enthusiasm was prodigious'.[3] **[fig. 2].**

The Bath performance came at a time when Dickens' life was being pulled in other directions, and he was not in the best of health himself. He was in the process of major alterations to his house in London; his tenth child would be born in 1852 despite the ill health of his wife and the tragic death of his ninth child, Dora, in 1851; his father had also died recently. He had also started up, was editing and contributing to the journal *Household Words,* and later *All the Year Round,* whilst maintaining his own writing career and beginning the public readings of his works that would prove so popular round the world. Perhaps the reception of the production at Bath confirmed his view of a city in decline. Certainly by his last visit he viewed the city as a 'mouldy old roosting-place'[4] and implied that the dead had taken possession of it[5] – although he also admitted to being 'bilious and uncomfortable' during that visit, so maybe he was just having a bad day.

On the surface this ticket is a simple, if decorative, memento of Dickens' performance in Bath, but, like so many items in the Library collections, it has a hidden history that helps illuminate life in the city at the time.

Notes

1.   William Lowndes, *They came to Bath* (Redcliffe, 1982), p.29
2.   Graham Storey, Kathleen Tillotson, Nina Burgis (eds), *The letters of Charles Dickens Volume 6 : 1850-1852,* (Clarendon, Oxford: 1988), letter to Henry Austin, November 13th 1851.
3.   *The Bath Chronicle,* November 13th 1851.
4.   Graham Storey (ed), *The letters of Charles Dickens, Volume 12 : 1868-1870,* (Clarendon, Oxford: 2002), letter to Miss Georgina Hogarth, January 29th 1869.
5.   *The letters of Charles Dickens Volume 12, letter to Viscount Torrington,* January 29th 1869.

Gustav Horstmann: Economic Migrant and Clock and Watchmaker, 1828-1893.

Stuart Burroughs

Whilst migration of populations across northern Europe has been a fact of life for centuries, they have historically been considered as mass movements with generalised explanations for why individuals would leave places of birth for a new life elsewhere presented. On closer inspection the masses of humanity on the move have been made up of individuals and each would have had their own, personal, reasons overlaying national or regional circumstances. Whilst the example of Gustav Horstmann might be considered in this essay as a typical case of an economic migrant, given the situation in his homeland, conjecture on his personal motivation is possible. Certainly his activities after arrival in this country make an interesting case study and reveal something about the attitudes at the time to arrivals from Central Europe and how they might progress or be prevented from progressing, commercially or socially. **[fig. 1]**.

Frederick Gustav Adolph Horstmann, known in the family as Gustav, was born in Oesterweg, Westphalia in Prussia in 1828. His father was a primary school teacher in a small community, who, interestingly, cultivated mulberry trees in the school grounds which he used to produce silk.[1] Gustav Horstmann was one of ten children, two of whom died in infancy. After a conventional upbringing he began an apprenticeship, at the age of fourteen, as a jeweller and watchmaker. In fact the four surviving sons all entered this trade. The apprenticeship involved learning and travelling with an established craftsman and progressing, through experience to the status of 'journeyman'. Journeyman is a term to distinguish a craftsman from an apprentice at one level and a master craftsman at another, it is used particularly in the clock and watchmaking field. Horstmann had been apprenticed to a famous watchmaker Louis-Clement Dejean, in Geneva[2], an arrangement having been made to have the teen-aged apprentice travel across the Alps. The fact that from an early age Horstmann was travelling away from home, to another state for work reasons,

Facing: fig 1: Portrait of Frederick Gustav Adolph Horstmann (1828-1893)
Founder of G. Horstmann & Sons.
Museum of Bath at Work Collection

may have removed any initial anxiety about his leaving home. In fact, over the succeeding ten or so years, Horstmann travelled across the continent working in the German states, Switzerland and possibly France. The borders of the emerging national states of Central Europe were still fluid at this stage which must have aided continental movement. An interesting fact which may have had some influence on Horstmann's later activities was that Dejean had himself been apprenticed to the highly inventive watchmaker, Abraham-Louis Breguet, whose speciality had been, in early nineteenth century Switzerland, self-winding watches or 'perpetuelles'.[3] These fob watches wound themselves by the movement of the wearer.

Despite travelling across Europe, Westphalia was still home to Gustav Horstmann but regional political circumstances in Prussia and the German states were, throughout the first half of the nineteenth century, forcing many inhabitants to move to more peaceful and stable states. Since the upheavals of the Napoleonic War, the rulers of the loose confederation of German princely states had wrestled with nationalist uprisings demanding change and the relaxations of the authority of autocratic monarchs. Repressive measures and anti-socialist laws in Prussia, to suppress such uprisings in 1820, had caused widespread alarm and the government's inability to deal with economic problems encouraged political radicals, followed many other citizens, to leave. In 1848, a major uprising in Berlin, encouraged by a revolution across Europe, failed within a year and was brutally supressed. By 1858, 1,000,000 people had emigrated from the German states and many of those had headed west to Britain or to the United States. In 1860 an immigrant to the United States was interviewed about his motivation to leave.

' I would prefer the civilised cultured Germany to Britain if it were only in its former orderly condition but as it has turned out recently and with the threatening prospect for the future I prefer Britain. Here I can live a more quiet and undisturbed life.'[4]

Certainly, Britain offered safety and stability and was relatively close geographically. Migration from the continent had a long tradition and in the main arrivals, with skills and ambition, were welcomed. Good links with the German states dated at least as far back as the accession to the British throne of

George 1 of the Hanoverians in 1714, and by 1810, there was a considerable German colony in London, with German language newspapers, and German businesses, well established across the country. By 1871, nearly 33,000 Germans were registered British citizens. Britain had escaped the turmoils of 1848 virtually unscathed and its reputation as a dynamic economic power was demonstrated, as if it needed to be, by the organisation and hosting of the display of manufactures at the Great Exhibition of the Works of Industry of All Nations, held in London in 1851. An additional attraction to those looking for a safe home, was that Great Britain was, by contrast to many of its continental neighbours, a politically liberal state.

Gustav Horstmann, having achieved 'journeyman' status by 1850, and keen to work independently, must have felt that his ambition to prosper commercially in his own country, let alone any other considerations, was being compromised to such an extent he might consider emigration. Later, when in Bath, Horstmann would claim he had been awarded a silver medal at the competition held in Brunswick in 1850 and this success may have given him further encouragement and confidence in his abilities. Incidentally, no information has ever been uncovered regarding a public competition or exhibition at Brunswick in that year.[5] It may have been an award for good service from an employer. Whatever the motivation, Gustav Horstmann seems to have rejected the option of moving to a neighbouring state, like France or Switzerland. Perhaps the 'pull factors' attracting him to Great Britain outweighed other considerations. Certainly, moving to a country he had no experience of (as far as we know) must have been a major step, leaving home, family and the culture of Central Europe for a completely new life. Whether he had decided to move permanently, from the outset, we may never know. However, until his marriage in 1858 it must have remained an option.

By the early 1850s, Gustav Horstmann had taken a position at the prestigious London clock and watchmaking business of Dwerrihouse & Company of Berkeley Square.[6] Presumably contacts in continental Europe had arranged an introduction and the reputation of Prussian watchmakers was high. The apprenticeship with Dejean must have played a part in his appointment. One wonders at Horstmann's standard of spoken English at this time. In travelling on mainland Europe he may have been able to survive with German or French. Having been appointed at Dwerrihouse & Company, Horstmann would have experienced the running of an established business and whilst practice in Britain would not have differed markedly from continental practice, he must have had to learn fast. Certainly, language schools existed in London to teach emigrants usable English and, again, any introduction arranged through contacts on the continent may have ensured accommodation and a friendly welcome from the German community.

Horstmann's activities in London are little known but after his move to Bath in or around 1856, he advertised himself as having been foreman at Dwerrihouse & Company. This position within the company suggests that the journeyman was not only experienced at the technical skills involved but capable of administration and job and staff management. Being a foreman must have given him greater confidence in his own abilities in Great Britain.

Around 1856, Horstmann moved from London and entered a short-lived business partnership with Arthur Robinson, in small premises at the rear of the Assembly Rooms, 4 The Collonnade, in Bennett Street.[7] The Collonnade was a row of small boutiques, almost booths arranged along the north side of the Assembly Rooms. They were destroyed when the building was bombed in 1942 and never replaced. The reasons for the move to Bath are again largely conjecture but it may be that having experience of working for a larger business had encouraged him, with experience under his belt, to strike out on his own.

Although Bath's position as a fashionable spa city had declined after 1800, its population continued to grow and it remained a city of well above national average wealth per head of population. By 1850 it had become increasingly favoured as a place of genteel retirement for the affluent rather than as a playground for the fashionable.

Watchmakers and jewellers had flourished in the city, some of them foreign, and as well as supplying fob watches and mantlepiece clocks an interest in complicated and precision timekeepers was the preserve of the wealthier population of the city. Geographically, the better clock and watchmakers were established on Milsom and George Streets by this time, and those businesses, like Horstmann and Robinson's, were on the edge of this area although close to the wealthy households of the Circus and Lansdown.

Once again, it is presumed that an introduction through contacts in London, possibly through Dwerrihouse, had been made for Horstmann in Bath. Given that Robinson does not appear prior to 1857 in Post Office Directories, it is even possible that they travelled down, having worked or known one another, in London to set up a small business in the thriving spa city. If this is not the case then Horstmann would have been sharing premises with a complete stranger who may have invited a partner to join a fledgling business. Whether the business was a partnership is unknown but unlikely. It is more likely the two were colleagues working with little in the way of resources on small shared premises. Whatever the reasons for the joint occupation, the arrangement does not seem to have been a success as by 1858 Robinson had disappeared.

In June 1858 Horstmann was married to Louisa Priscilla Knott, who lived locally, and it is worthwhile considering this in some detail as apart from anything else it suggests that Horstmann had decided to make Great Britain his home. Given that Horstmann had not been living in Bath more than eighteen months or so before the marriage, one wonders how the two met, and how the prospect of marrying into an English family was considered by Horstmann and how marrying a German in fairly quick time was considered by the Knott family, not least the bride's father. Quite where the two had met is guesswork. The Knott family were resident at 3 Circus Place, a few minutes walk from 4 The Collonnades, and it is possible that Horstmann repaired a watch or clock for the family; or the couple met on the street. We do not know where Horstmann was staying at this time, it might even be that he was lodging with the Knotts (which would explain a great deal!), but assuming not, it is possible that they may have met at church.[8] The couple were married at St. Swithin's church Walcot, one of the nearest churches to Circus Place, the shop at the Collonnades, and it is most likely that Horstmann would have lodgings close to the business somewhere in the Walcot Street area.

Interestingly, Louisa Knott's father was not registered at 3 Circus Place home as the householder during the 1850s.[9] Instead his wife, Maria Knott , a lace cleaner was the household head with several small children and her own mother were all living there. Louisa's father, John Stuart Knott, may have been lodging in Bristol and working as a pastry cook. Shortly after the marriage in June 1858, when he signed the marriage certificate, John Knott died and his death was registered in Bedminster where he may have been working and living. It is possible that Louisa's parents were separated or that he was compelled to work and live in Bristol by financial circumstances. If the death of John Knott followed illness and death was foretold, it is quite possible that this encouraged Louisa Knott and the family to consider marriage more urgently to an ambitious and dynamic watch and clockmaker. This in the hope that Louisa's fortunes at least would be more assured, notwithstanding the groom being an immigrant to Bath and the country. This appreciation might explain the short courtship before marriage and there is no record of any ill-feeling about the union in any of the family records or recollections of this time.

By 1858, the business with Robinson had folded and an advertisement appeared in the *Universal Bath Guide*, announcing the independent business, and his arrival from Geneva via the Foremanship at Dwerrihouse & Co. In 1861, Horstmann moved business premises and had made a home for his family at 5 Prince's Buildings on George Street. There were domestic premises above the shop and in the 1861 census, Gustav and Louisa were recorded with their first infant child, Ida, who had been born early that year. Also registered were Thomas Newman, 'an apprentice machinist', and Elisabeth Gregory, 'a servant'.[10] It is possible that the success of Horstmann's business to this point, to the extent of taking on a whole shop much closer to the commercial centre of the city, allowed them to afford the luxury of a servant and possibly an apprentice to Gustav Horstmann, both of whom were living with the family. If this was the case the trade must have been improving. It may be that these two were simply sharing the domestic accommodation above the shop but this seems less likely. Most interestingly of all is the presence of Henrik (recorded by the enumerator) as Henry Horstmann staying at the home. Henrik was Gustav's youngest brother, and whilst all four Horstmann brothers became jewellers and watchmakers, only these two moved to England. Henrik is registered as an apprentice and it seems likely that this seventeen year old had followed his brother to England, once he had been established, and was working with him as another apprentice. Latterly Henrik Horstmann left Bath and set up a watch and clockmaking business in Weston-super-Mare. During the same census, Henrik was also recorded as having been a lodger at the Knott family home at 3 Circus Place! It suggests that he was moving between the two addresses during the census was being taken and hence recorded twice - a most unusual occurrence.

By 1864, the business and home had moved again, only a short distance to 3 Bladud's Buildings, slightly further from the centre of Bath. By this time the family had grown with the birth of two sons, Gustav Otto and Frederick. It may be that the move was prompted by the enlarged family or the prospect of larger business premises, the address may have been better appointed with larger window space for example.

In addition to the running of the growing business, Horstmann began the development of a series of devices which may have begun as work required by his own business, but that suggests perhaps he was keen to break out of the confines of the horological trade to something greater.

In 1865, *The English Mechanic* magazine staged a competition for the production of the most accurate machine for measuring the smallest item.[11] Horstmann entered a small measuring machine, of his own invention, which won First Prize. The machine, the original of which is in the possession of the The Science Museum, would have been the sort of instrument a watch maker might have used to measure the smallest components for watches. Horstmann's name is, however, almost unknown in the history of measuring technology as other prominent inventors had, or would later produce more accurate micrometers, so relegating this invention to a footnote in the development of such machinery. Certainly, despite the success there is no evidence of the machine being commercially exploited. Perhaps Horstmann had too many other things to contend with, like a young family and business to divert attention to the exploitation of the measuring machine, or perhaps he had no success attracting financial backing for its development. In any event, it appears only one example was ever made for display although its possible that at least one other example was used by Horstmann himself in his day-to-day work. [**fig.2**].

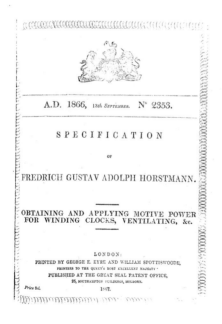

fig 2: Patent specification for Horstmann's heat-driven motor, 1866. Specification for obtaining and applying motive power for winding clocks, ventilating, &c.
Museum of Bath at Work Collection

The contrast in his approach to his next invention could not have been more striking. In September 1866, Horstmann applied for a provisional patent application for a heat-driven motor.[12] Perhaps inspired by the 'perpetual' watches of Breguet, Horstmann suggested in his patent, a motor, which could primarily be used to wind a clock, which, driven by changes in the ambient temperature would run perpetually, without winding. The Horstmann motor used a cylinder of volative (and potentially inflammable) liquid and variations in temperature around the cylinder (for example during night and day or between a hot day and a following cool day) caused changes in the pressure within. These changes were used to drive a piston in a pressurised system which in turn affected small movements. Although Horstmann's prime application for this 'motor' was in the winding of a clock, he also envisaged it being used to open or shut windows or the damper of a domestic grate. In essence, the point at which the pressure changed inside the cylinder worked like a thermostat, producing physical work on window hinges or the winding barrel of a clock. Unfortunately despite much attention, then and since, only a handful of clocks were made and it is unclear as to whether any other applications were made for sale. Sidney Horstmann, Gustav's youngest son born in 1881, claimed that a system to operate the windows of the family home and a clock had been installed by his father, and that the temperature regulation provided by the opening and shutting of the windows prevented sufficient variation of temperature within the house which stopped the clock! This may or may not have been the case and if so it is the only evidence for such a system having been installed anywhere.

In contrast to his work on his micrometer, Horstmann patented this idea and evidently hoped to commercially exploit it. Unfortunately, leaks in the pressurised system were common causing the clocks to stop. The reason why Horstmann could not attract financial backing to develop or improve the invention, or licencing it to another manufacturer, may have been a result of this unreliability. In addition the presence of containers of inflammable liquid, required to drive the motor, in a home were a fire risk and the pressure leaks in the faulty system releasing inflammable gas into the air! These safety considerations may have doomed attempts to market the invention for domestic use. However, Horstmann continued to try to develop the motor and, as late as 1885, a stall at the International Inventions Fair at London was booked by Horstmann for a demonstration of his 'Thermo-auto Motor'. The stall comprised a self winding clock, the 'Thermo-automotor Ventilator' and 'an apparatus showing the amount of weight that can be raised by the Thermo-auto Motor'.[13] The fact that decades after the patent application Horstmann was still attempting to interest other businesses in the invention, shows that he hoped the technical shortcomings might be conquered.

Is it possible that racial prejudice had a part in the failure to attract backing for the device in the 1860s? This seems unlikely as, although there was some anti-Prussian feeling in Britain following the expansionist activities of Prussia against Denmark and Austria in the 1860s, Horstmann was by this time quite well established in Bath and his name was well known after the award of the English Mechanic prize in 1865. More likely is that the unreliability under test, and the failure over many years to make the system work properly, has seen the Thermo-auto Motor as an interesting curiosity rather than a world-changing engine.

By 1866, Horstmann was employing four members of staff at the shop, and in 1871, the census records the Horstmann family in rooms above the Bladud's Buildings shop. Four of the five children were recorded, Ida, Gustav Otto, Frederick and Albert (born 1869). A fifth child, Ernst, born in 1866, was missing and it is possible he was staying with relatives and may have even been ill.[14] He reappeared in later records. In 1876, the business moved to larger premises at 7 George Street and the scale and scope of the business had considerably increased. In addition to clock and watchmaking the firm was undertaking optician's and jewellery work. In addition, Horstmann was charging £80.00 each year for the winding and regulation of ten clock and school clocks. These included Bath Abbey's clock and carillon.[15]

In 1881, the business moved to its final home at 13 Union Street in the centre of the city. Not only were these premises much larger but the domestic accommodation for the family was for the first time separate. [**fig. 3**]. In the same year the family were registered as living at 4 Vale View Place.[16] Interestingly, in the census of that year, Gustav has been recorded by the enumerator as Thomas G. A. Horstmann.[17] Presumably, this is an error in the recording possibly due to the foreign accent that Horstmann still retained. It seems unlikely that Horstmann had deliberately changed his own name for the record, but it does raise the interesting question of how far immigrants were and are willing to go to fit in with the indigenous population by adapting their names. It would seem that by this time, given the business's success, that such

fig 3: Staff outside the Horstmann premises, c.1900. The business was located at 13 Union Street, Bath from 1881.
Museum of Bath at Work Collection

effort was unnecessary. Frederick Horstmann (aged 14) is recorded as 'a jeweller's apprentice'. An advertisement for the business in 1881 still refered to 'the inventor and patentee of the self winding clock and clocks wound by the year.'[18] **[fig. 4].**

A number of photographs survive of the Union Street shop taken in the early twentieth century and, although they include services that the business may have offered subsequent to Gustav Horstmann death, they give a good idea of the range of work being undertaken through the painted advertisement on the plate glass shop window. These comprised optical prescriptions, watches and clock repairs, battery recharging, electroplating and gilding and the making and repair of plate and jewellery.

The firm flourished through the 1880s and, in 1889, a reference was made to Horstmann having worked with a F.W. Austin 'in repairing and manufacturing on the premises which we have the latest and most improved

fig 4: Horstmann's self-winding clock. This example can still be seen working at the Museum of Bath at Work.

Photograph – Daniel Brown

tools and appliances of English, Swiss, German and American makes'.[19] Quite who Mr.F.W. Austin was is not known but he must have been of some fame. By 1889, four of the sons were helping run the business which by this time was operating as G. Horstmann & Sons and was not only well established but continuing to expand. From the family home at 34 Brock Street (where they had moved to in 1888) a milliners business was being run by 'The misses Horstmann & Knott'. This short-lived business was run by Augusta Horstmann and Louisa's youngest sister, Catharine. Frederick Horstmann's son, also called Frederick, recalled Augusta's artistic flair, and she was responsible for the portraits of Gustav and Louisa painted in the early 1890s.[20]

In 1892, Gustav Horstmann proudly announced in an advertisement in the *Bath Postal Directory* that:

> 'During 1891 seven certificates were awarded by the British Horological Institution in London to members of our staff – two for watch making and five for clock making. This record has not been equalled by any firm in England. With these qualifications we are prepared to undertake the repair of the most delicate and complicated horological instruments.'[21]

It must have been heartening at this stage to review his company's successes with such satisfaction. Four sons were running the business and developing and expanding the shop's range of services. After their father's death the firm would go on to greater success. Sidney Horstmann, born in 1881, recalled having been taught by a private tutor until the age of twelve, at which point he attended a commercial school in Northampton Street. Sidney Horstmann was the only son not to follow the others into the horological business.

On April 9th 1893, Gustav Horstmann died, at the age of 65, after a stroke had caused partial paralysis. An obituary in the Horological Institute recorded that he was:

> 'the inventor of several ingenious contrivances amongst them a self winding clock which attracted considerable attention some years ago. He had for some time been suffering from paralysis but no immediate danger was apprehended until two days before his decease. Mr. Horstmann will be succeeded by his sons

who have been in partnership with him for some years. They are known to readers of the journal as holders of first class certificates from the Horological Institute.'[22]

Louisa Horstmann lived until 1904, by which time the Horstmann sons had done more than continue the successful clock and watchmakers, they had laid the foundations for two much more famous family businesses that survive, however altered, into our own time. **[fig. 5]**.

fig 5: G. Horstmann & Sons billhead, 1910. By Appointment to H.M. Office of Works. *Museum of Bath at Work Collection*

In 1904, The Horstmann Gear Company was formed to exploit an automatic gear box invented by Sidney Horstmann. When this failed, Sidney Horstmann formed the Horstmann Car Company and the other sons continued, using the Horstmann Gear Company name, to exploit a number of highly successful industrial clocks and timeswitches for automatic control. Whilst the car production ceased in 1928, Sidney Horstmann continued an engineering business, becoming Horstman Defence Systems Ltd. The Horstmann Gear Company survives, operating in Bristol as Horstmann Timers.

It is useful to review the career and life of Gustav Horstmann, not least because he had died before the much greater commercial successes of his sons had become apparent. From a travelling apprentice in mid-nineteenth century Europe to emigré journeyman in Victorian London, and from failed inventor but reliable and successful businessman, the story is an individual one. It would be appropriate to suggest that the inventive flair of Horstmann's sons had been encouraged by their father and that through that they managed to achieve what

fig 6: Horstmann's sons in a family group, c.1920s. The sons expanded the business following the death of their father in 1893.
Museum of Bath at Work Collection

he had not, to break out of the traditional field of horology into the general field of precision engineering and make Horstmann a household name. During his time in England, Horstmann seems to have managed to slip easily into the business community and there is no evidence that he ever suffered more upset through being an immigrant than his name being regularly mis-recorded by census enumerators.

Ironically, it was the outbreak of the First World War, some twenty years after Gustav Horstmann's death, that the anti-German feeling he had escaped was visited upon his sons. In 1915 the Horstmann Gear Company successfully sued[23] the British Home, Foreign and Colonial Automatic Lighting Control Co. for libel - when the latter accused the Horstmann brothers of being 'the King's enemies', and in 1921 the Horstmann Car Co. removed the second 'n' from the company name to remove associations with the recently defeated enemy. Sidney Horstmann felt the Horstman car would have a better chance of sales in western Europe after insinuations and accusations were aimed at him and the company.

Notes

1. Chris Davis, *The Horstmanns of Bath*, unpublished MS., (2008).
2. Ian White,*Watch and Clock Makers in the City of Bath*, (1996).
3. *Encyclopaedia Brittanica*, (1959).
4. Unidentified Prussian Migrant, *United States Office of Statistics*, (1860).
5. Ian White, *Watch and Clock Makers in the City of Bath*.
6. Ian White, *Watch and Clock Makers in the City of Bath*.
7. *Bath Postal Directory*, 1858-9.
8. Chris Davis, *The Horstmann of Bath*, unpublished MS.,(2008).
9. *Bath Postal Directories*, 1852-9.
10. Great Britain Census, 1861.
11. Jean Manco, *Southbank Villas, An Historical Survey of Premises latterly occupied by Horstmann Gear Co.* (2005).
12. British Patent No 2353. September 13th 1866.
13. Application to exhibit at International Inventions Exhibition London, 1885.
14. Great Britain Census, Walcot parish, Bath, 1871.
15. Invoice from Gustav Horstmann 1876-1881, Museum of Bath at Work.
16. *Bath Postal Directory*, 1877.
17. Great Britain Census, Walcot parish, 1881.
18. *Post Office Directory*, 1882.
19. *Bath Post Office Directory*,1882.
20. Frederick Horstmann. Unpublished MS., 1971, Museum of Bath at Work.
21. *Horological Journal*, 1891.
22. *Horological Journal*, May 1893.
23. *Keene's Bath Journal*, February 15th 1915.

Crime and Criminal Portraits in Victorian and Edwardian Bath

Graham Davis

There have always been crimes and criminals since time immemorial, but the modern notions of crime and the practice of modern policing, outside the metropolis, came in the early Victorian period. The concept of a 'criminal class', or what became known as the Victorian underworld, owed something to contemporary ideas on social hierarchy. The criminal class was to be found at the base of society. *Frazer's Magazine* in June 1832 reported the existence of a new and well-organised criminal class. Its members thrived on the certainties of making substantial gains while the chances of being caught were fairly remote.[1]

The modern distinction between the fear of crime and known levels of criminality in society were evident throughout the nineteenth century. These increased in intensity through a series of 'moral panics', fuelled by newspaper hysteria, and were commonly followed by an increase in police powers or regulation by the state in a seemingly inexorable march towards what has been dubbed 'a surveillance society'.[2]

As is well known, the first professional police force introduced in England was the Metropolitan Police force in London in 1829 by the Home Secretary, Sir Robert Peel (hence the nicknames of uniformed police as 'peelers' or 'bobbies').[3] Provincial forces followed after the Municipal Corporations Act of 1835, with incorporated boroughs having powers to establish borough police forces. The Bath Police force was early off the mark when established in January 1836. Nationally, as Stanley Palmer has shown, it was the fear of Chartist activity, in the period 1836 to 1848, and the threat of disorder that prompted many northern cities to set up their own forces.[4] County forces followed legislation in 1856 to allow the policing of rural areas. The fear of lawlessness was also fuelled by the rapid growth of urban populations, driven by industrialisation. The Reform riots in Bristol and Nottingham in 1831 prompted fears among the authorities that the sheer size of towns was creating a worrying separation of the classes. The result was that whole districts of towns became centres of poverty and moral destitution, with a complete absence of moral supervision by the respectable

Facing: Detail of Portrait of Henry Thompson, 1907
A representation of a stereotypical criminal face.
Bath Record Office, Bath & North East Somerset Council

99

middle classes, who were moving to the leafy suburbs.[5] Crime and poverty were seen as defining characteristics of inner-city slum districts.

Edwin Chadwick's monumental report on the sanitary condition of the great cities, published in 1842, had shown that crime, poverty and disease were seen as inevitable companions.[6] However, it was the pioneering work of the journalist, Henry Mayhew and his assistants, who brought to vivid life the street people of the metropolis in a series of memorable interviews during the 1850s.[7] Middle-class readers of *The Morning Post* were treated to vicarious accounts of the lives of street traders, petty criminals and prostitutes in London. These accounts, interspersed with heavy moral condemnation by Mayhew, confirmed respectable people in the view that there was a substratum of society that was as alien to them as the savage tribes of distant continents. Crime was understood in terms of a moral framework. Further incidents, such as the garrotting panic and Fenian outrages in the 1860s and the infamous Whitechapel Murders, committed by 'Jack the Ripper' in the 1880s, contributed to public alarm and led to increased police powers.

Adding to the certain belief in the existence of a criminal class at the base of society was the increasing popularity of the pseudo-science of physiognomy. This was especially influential in the 1860s in Britain and America. At its centre, was the belief that certain physical characteristics denoted criminal tendencies. Hence the fascination with the measurement of skulls, the shape of the jaw, the shape and length of noses and the angle of the forehead.[8] Charles Darwin's publication of *The Origin of Species,* in 1859, gave a certain credence to the belief in various stages of human evolution, with some nations and some people regarded as more advanced than others.

The alleged simian features of Irish revolutionaries were depicted in *Punch* cartoons by Tenniel and remain a subject of continuing scholarly controversy.[9] A recent biography of Tenniel also shows how unflattering depictions of working-class stereotypes were commonly deployed in Victorian cartoons, appealing to the all-too-evident class prejudice of the time.[10]

§

Crime in Bath

The streets of early, nineteenth-century Bath were plagued by juvenile gangs, hawkers and street sellers of every description, and most notoriously by beggars. The noise and disorder were wholly out of keeping with its reputation as a quiet resort for the invalid and elderly among its residents. In the 1820s and 1830s, Bath was appealing to a new clientele of middle-class visitors and new residents to replace the loss of the fashionable company in its Georgian heyday. A contemporary complaint, in satirical verse, listed some of the cries that assaulted the senses of visitors from street sellers, chairmen, chimney sweeps, coal-dealers and fruit women, who all vied with each other for public attention, and created a chorus of ill-assorted sounds in the streets. Most feared and despised were the beggars:

> 'I always have heard that the provident mayor
> Had a terrific rod to make beggars beware;
> But I find to my cost, they infest ev'ry street –
> First, a boy with one eye, - then a man without feet,
> Who cleverly stumps upon two patten rings, -
> One bellows, one whispers, one snuffles, one sings; -
> From Holloway's garrets and cellars they swarm;
> But I'll pause, - on this subject I'm growing too warm.'[11]

The establishment of a borough police force in Bath in 1836, under the central direction of the Watch Committee and the Chief Constable, provided the city with a single authority, and took on a closer regulation of street activity as an important function of police duties.

> 'The Watchmen, too, are all dispersed,
> And Bath with new Police is curs'd,
> Commanded by a sturdy tar,
> Who'd rule – as in a man of war –
> For C——l keeps 'em all in check,
> As on his own quarter-deck,
> Now – if a beggar asks a groat,
> A fellow, in a smart blue coat,
> Stalks up, and orders him away,
> Although, perhaps, he starves that day;
> For begging here a perfect trade is –
> Supported chiefly by the ladies,'[12]

These features were not to disappear from the streets of Victorian Bath, but were undoubtedly brought within a more acceptable level after the establishment of regular day and night patrolling of the city streets. In this regard, Bath shared in the common experience of Victorian cities in improving public order. However, unlike the great industrial cities, where, in addition to some full-time criminals, there were also juveniles who took to crime only as a secondary occupation, in towns such as Bath, the typical juvenile criminal looked to crime alone for his livelihood.[13] Poverty, loss of parents, lack of education and a shortage of employment in the city created conditions favourable to the development of juvenile crime:

> 'George Kingston,under 14, charged with stealing a tin canister and 7s. in money belonging to Jane Collet of Abbey Green. She keeps a coal shed and employs the boy. He took off with the money. The prisoner was one of that unfortunate class of children, uneducated, uncared for, destined to become criminals. He had already been in prison, and his father was in the Workhouse. According to his mother, the boy finds a refuge at night "in passages, or where he can!" He was convicted and sentenced to 14 days hard labour, and to be once whipped,'[14]

In the 1850s and 1860s, as Bath attracted fewer visitors, the extent of juvenile and other crimes appeared to decline. At Bath Quarter Sessions in 1864, the small number and petty nature of crimes committed gave rise to expressions of satisfaction. Only ten prisoners were before the Recorder and five of them stood charged with robbing their lodgings. Such persons were generally poor and any theft was due to the embarrassment of having no food, they took what was readily to hand, often with the expectation of being able to redeem the things without despoiling the owners.[15]

With the revival in the numbers of visitors in the last twenty years of the century, there was an accompanying increase in the presence of tramps, beggars and prostitutes in the city.[16] The level and structure of criminal activity in Bath was closely associated with the city's prosperity. This was not always appreciated at the time, but with hindsight it is clear that crime was an integral part of Bath's function as a resort. Moreover, in an economy where traditional employment was being lost in trades such as shoemaking and clothmaking, more working people were compelled to make a living on the streets as hawkers and costermongers. The move-on policy of police control in the central commercial streets threatened the livelihood of the urban poor and was a continual source of conflict. The police also focussed attention on working-class districts, where closer regulation of lodging-houses, pubs, and popular forms of recreation was enforced by a uniformed authority. Working-class hostility towards the police stemmed from a challenge to a traditional way of life.

Benjamin Disraeli's famous dictum, 'lies, damned lies and statistics' applies with full force in relation to criminal statistics in Victorian Bath as well as in our own time.[17]

The two primary sources, the Petty Sessions and Chief Constable's Reports can merely provide a broad framework. Petty offences formed the great bulk of known criminal activity. For the year 1852, a total of 1,412 offences, a miscellaneous category, offences against the Borough Bye-Laws ranked highest with 276 or a fifth of the total. These included offences such as obstructions of the footway by the baskets of streetsellers, carts left unattended, ale houses left open after hours, and non-payment of rates, so confirming the importance of police supervision of the public streets. A characteristic example follows:

> 'Charlotte Perry summoned for assaulting Elizabeth Davis in Avon Street. The parties are fruit women, and a dispute arose between them on a rival claim to occupy a place under the arch leading from Cheap Street to the Abbey Churchyard, for the sale of fruit. According to the evidence which was given by several loquacious females, both complainant and defendant indulged freely in the use of the vulgar tongue. After a patient hearing of the most conflicting evidence, which disclosed on both sides conduct discreditable to the sex, the magistrates ordered each party to find bail to keep the peace for seven days.'[18]

Closely related were offences related to various forms of drunkenness – escalating from drunk and disorderly, drunk and incapable to drunk and riotous. As the Temperance lobby never failed to point out, drink was also identified with many crimes over and above the number of drunkenness offences.[19] In 1852, the latter numbered 242 or (17.1 per cent of the total), but drink was also commonly associated with common assaults. These amounted to 218 offences or (15.4 per cent). Larceny, including all forms of petty theft and embezzlement, totalled 195 offences (13.8 per cent of the total). Closely behind came begging with 192 cases or (13.6 per cent), almost certainly a decline on the amount of begging recorded earlier in the century when it was of legendary proportions. The remainder of offences formed a miscellaneous grouping, including some of recent origin: workhouse offences, cruelty to animals, damage to property, breaches of the peace and offences related to prostitution.

Some comparisons can be made with the figures recorded in the Chief Constable's Reports from later in the century. A measure of the extent of crime, known and acted on by the police, can be taken in terms of the number of persons proceeded against in relation to the population of Bath. This measure produces a remarkably constant figure – 2.6 per cent in 1852, 2.7 per cent in the period 1878 to 1883 and 2.4 per cent between 1886 and 1894. However, the figures are seriously misleading. In the period, 1878 to 1894, a substantial proportion of cases came under a new heading of offences against the Elementary Education Act, the failure of parents to send their children to school. Before the 1870s, there was no such legal requirement for parents and therefore no recorded offences. It is a classic case of new legislation seriously distorting the pattern of criminal offences. For purposes of comparison, education offences need to be excluded. When this is done, the extent of prosecutions appears to be reduced by half from 2.6 per cent to 1.3 per cent. Indictable offences were also included in the totals for the later period, so disguising the extent of the reduction. The conclusion must be that there was a significant fall in the number of prosecutions for comparable offences in Bath in the second half of the century. This almost certainly meant a corresponding reduction in the level of criminal activity in the city.

This was in line with the national pattern, that after a probable increase in crime in the first half of the century, particularly in juvenile crime, there was a reduction in the incidence of crime in the period after 1850.[20]

A similar reduction occurred in the number of persons conveyed to gaol in the 1880s and 1890s compared with the 1840s. The average annual number of persons committed for trial and summarily convicted in Bath for the years 1842 to 1849 amounted to 636.[21] Between 1886 and 1894, the average numbers sent to gaol had fallen to 198.[22] Changes in sentencing policy, and a lower proportion of convictions ending in prison sentences, distorted these comparative figures. Debtors, for instance, were no longer imprisoned so frequently in the later period. This, in part, explains the reduction in numbers conveyed to gaol, but the scale of the reduction reinforces the conclusion that the level of comparable criminal activity had declined substantially.

Vagrants, however, were an exception to the general rule. In the 1840s, the authorities were alarmed at the annual influx of 5,000 tramps admitted to the Union Workhouse. Contemporaries regarded them as part of the criminal classes, 'a highly dangerous set of persons (travelling) over the country passing their nights at workhouses, and their days in begging, stealing, and drunkenness'.[23] Despite the efforts made to restrict their numbers, they came in increasing numbers in the closing decades of the century – 4-5,000 in the 1880s rising to 7-9,000 in the 1890s.[24] With the Workhouse unable to accommodate such numbers, alternatives were found in the Refuges for the Destitute and in the city's registered and unregistered lodging houses, concentrated in the poorest areas of the city. On any one night, there were likely to be a hundred or more lodgers in the registered lodging houses in Avon Street alone.[25] Against this background prison served as an overspill for vagrants.

Other trends identified between offences, committed in 1852 and in the 1880s and 1890s, show a decline in levels of drunkenness that fit in with the national pattern of a peak of beer consumption in the 1870s.[26] The prosecution of drunkenness offences of various kinds totalled 242 in 1852 but had fallen to 60 or 70 by the 1880s. A more tolerant attitude on the part of the police may explain some of the reduction, but a movement of population away from the inner city to the suburbs could also have been responsible. The number of inns remained high, increasing from 208 to 243 between 1860 and 1900, while the number of beershops declined from 21 to 1 in the same period.[27] Allied to drunkenness offences was a decline in the number of common assaults, falling from 218 in 1852 to 143 in 1883. Larceny cases had a more pronounced decline, from 195 in 1852 to 57 in 1883. What these changes suggest is that a stricter system of law and order was in place by the later Victorian period. The Police, armed with wider powers, had become less tolerant of street offences of all kinds, with the result that the central streets of Bath would have become quieter and safer places for respectable citizens than at mid-century.

Criminal photographs and record keeping

In addition to increased powers for the police that included the introduction of finger printing, plain-clothes detectives, and the establishment of MI5 to combat the threat of Fenian violence, a new weapon in the fight against crime was presented with the development of photography. Police forces began to take photographs of prisoners and to circulate them around the country. The result was that by the 1880s, records began to be collected of criminal 'mugshots', usually in the form of full-face pictures, but also with occasional side-on shots. I came across a series of volumes in Bath Central Police Station in Manvers Street that contained several hundred photographs of criminals, usually appended to a page that listed the criminal record and a description of the individual in question.[28] The colour of hair, eyes, type of build, and distinguishing marks such as moles, scars and tattoos (both of the latter were very common) were all listed, plus details of occupation and birthplace. Some criminals operated under a number of aliases, as a means of avoiding being caught, so these were assiduously recorded alongside each known crime committed and where the system of justice had caught up with them.

What I found to be most interesting about the kind of criminals who came before local justices was that it became clear from the photographs that Victorian ideas of physiognomy were quite misplaced. While there were a few examples of 'rough-looking' characters and certainly evidence of poverty in the clothes they wore, the surprising conclusion was that many were good looking, well dressed, and would have clearly merged into respectable society. Most importantly, the conclusion reached was that crime in Bath was a reflection of the social and economic structure of its community. Bath, with its surfeit of wealthy women of mature years, attracted con artists who preyed on their loneliness and vulnerability.

§

Criminal Portraits

The photographs appear in the top corner of a page of information on the prisoner's criminal record as illustrated with the first case. A summary of the information provided is given so that focus can be concentrated on the faces and appearance of each of them.

fig 1: **Profile and Portrait of Henry Thompson, 1907.**
Photographed on the 22nd November, 1907.
Bath Record Office, Bath & North East Somerset Council

fig 2: **Portraits of Henry Thompson and criminal record, 1907.** A criminal record of over 20 years is listed.
Bath Record Office, Bath & North East Somerset Council

Henry Thompson [fig. 1 and fig. 2] is the first of a select few chosen to illustrate key patterns of criminality. His face-on and side-on photographs are a rare example of the physical characteristics Victorians associated with criminal types. His stunted stature, (5 ft. 1inch) the snub nose, and poor appearance, all mark him out as a stereotype criminal. His use of aliases – Harry Thompson and Harry Weeks – reveal a deliberate calculation to avoid arrest. Described as a labourer from Brecon, his first offence, committed at the age of 13, was the stealing of a rabbit. His punishment was a day in prison and six strokes. This was followed by stealing two iron wheels and the minor offence of playing pitch and toss. These were juvenile offences of no great significance, but he then got into more serious trouble with assaults on the Police, housebreaking, wounding, theft of money, drunkenness and being found on enclosed premises. These crimes were committed across a wide geographical territory – Cardiff, Plymouth, Rodborough, Gloucester, Exeter, Leicester, Wakefield, and finally in Bath. This was an unusual pattern for a labourer. Broadly, the cases suggest that the better-educated, higher-class criminals tended to move more widely than the common, petty thief. For most offences, the sentences were imprisonment with hard labour, but one offence led him to be sent to an asylum, which suggests that he may have suffered from mental ill-health. The association between drink and violence will come as no surprise to modern readers. In conclusion, Harry Thompson may be regarded as a classic recidivist, petty criminal. His long career in crime, lasting twenty years, points to the failure of the justice system in either deterring him or in reforming him away from future criminal acts.

fig 3: Profile and Portrait of William Jackson, 1904. A begger who feigned blindness.
Bath Record Office, Bath & North East Somerset Council

William Jackson [fig. 3] was more characteristic of criminals attracted to Bath. A native of the Rhondda, aged 34, 5 ft 6 inches in height, of medium build, dark brown hair (slightly bald) with brown eyes and a fresh complexion. He also had a large lump at the back of his neck and what looks in the photograph as evidence of scrofula on the side of his face. His record showed three offences of begging, in Oxford and in Bristol twice, but a revealing comment may be quoted in full: 'This man is a clever imposter + feigns Blindness and is led about by a dog. He was examined at Oxford by 5 doctors who found the Blindness was entirely feigned.' Even though there are no recorded instances of Jackson begging in Bath, it is quite likely that he would have tried his luck in the city. The Police were certainly made aware of his mode of operation and would have been on the look out for him. He received 5 days hard labour, then 14 days hard labour on the second and third offences.

Annie Nash [fig. 4], alias Annie Strain, a well-dressed young lady of 19 in 1912, represented the most common kind of female criminal. She was a domestic servant, one of a huge army of servants in Bath, who combined low wages with the opportunity to steal from employers. Being in the presence of a higher standard of living could only have added to temptation. She was described as 5 ft. 4 inches in height, of thin build, pale complexion, having black hair and brown eyes. She was born in West Lavington, near Devizes. The interesting feature of her record was that she began her career, stealing ten shillings, at the age of eleven in Bath. She spent a day in prison on promising to go to the Salvation Army Home. Eight years later, she was convicted of acquiring money

fig 4: Portrait of Annie Nash, 1904. A domestic servant, the most common occupation of female criminals.
Bath Record Office, Bath & North East Somerset Council

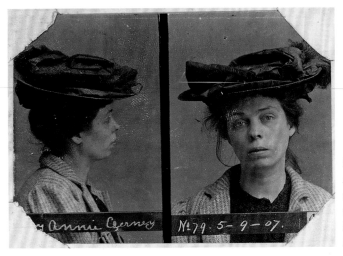

fig 5: **Profile and Portrait of Annie Cerney, 1907.** Another domestic servant, convicted of drink related offences.
Bath Record Office, Bath & North East Somerset Council

by false pretences in Bristol and then two offences of stealing rings and other things. She served three and six months in prison with hard labour.

Annie Cerney [fig. 5], alias Ellen Williams, was another domestic servant who had clearly followed a downward path over a period of eighteen years. This is reflected in her sad appearance in the photograph, taken in 1907 when she was 30 years old. A native of Bath, she was 5 ft. 1 inch tall, with light brown hair, blue eyes and a slim build. Her first offence of larceny occurred in Bath in 1892 when she was 15. She received one month in prison with hard labour. There followed four more similar offences of larceny when she used different names. Then in 1908, she was charged with being drunk in charge of a child in Bath and stealing a pair of boots. In 1910, she was convicted of five offences of being drunk and disorderly in Bath. These resulted in sentences of between 14 days and one month hard labour. Finally, the magistrates resolved to send her to a Home for two years in an attempt to ween her off the drink.

Annie Cerney's criminal career began as a young girl involved in theft from her employers. It took a turn for the worse when her drink problems became endemic. Her prospects may have improved with time spent in a home for inebriates. Otherwise, her future life would have been very bleak.

Jane and Annie Flint [fig. 6 and fig. 7], alias Jackson and Shaw, aged 65 and 30 in 1896, a mother and daughter combination, were professional con artists who toured the country, preying on religious sympathies. Jane was 5 ft 1 inch, of stoutish build, fresh complexion, with grey hair and brown eyes. Annie was 5ft 4 inches, well proportioned, with a pale face and full eyes. The record shows

fig 6: Portrait of Jane Flint, 1896. The mother and one half of a notorious pair of con artists. *Bath Record Office, Bath & North East Somerset Council*

fig 7: Portrait of Annie Flint, 1896. The daughter and the other half of a notorious pair of con artists. *Bath Record Office, Bath & North East Somerset Council*

that they were sentenced to three months hard labour for larceny at Leek in Staffordshire in 1896 and were wanted in many parts of the country for similar charges. Their *modus operandi* was to take lodgings and make themselves acquainted with the clergy, and join the Church Guild, and thus steal several articles. Bath, with its many religious charities, might well have been an obvious target for this notorious pair.

Tom Rostren Stewart [fig. 8], alias George Richard Brooks and Lees, was one of three examples of male con artists who, as sophisticated types of criminals, were especially attracted to Bath. In appearance, they were far removed from the likes of Henry Thompson, looking every inch members of respectable society and relying on an assumed social status and bearing, that put them beyond suspicion given the attitudes of contemporaries. A native of Bury in

fig 8: Portrait of Tom Rostren Stewart, undated. Con artist of respectable appearance.
Bath Record Office, Bath & North East Somerset Council

fig 9: Portrait of Samuel Zucker, 1903. Con artist with multiple aliases.
Bath Record Office, Bath & North East Somerset Council

Lancashire, aged 27, 5 ft. 5 inches in height, of medium build and having light brown hair, grey eyes and a fresh complexion, he was handsome and well-dressed. He could have been an actor which, of course in a criminal way, he was. Perhaps, surprisingly, his appearance was not without blemish. He had a scar in the centre of his forehead, a white mole near the corner of his eye and the bridge of his nose was broken. He also had scars on his fingers, right wrist and on both shins, a boil mark between his shoulders, 3 blue prison marks on his right thigh, and was suffering from scaly skin disease. He was brought before Bath Petty Sessions for the offence of false pretences. His father and brother were bound over in the sum of £20 each for 12 months. So he was bailed out by his family that had the means to find the required sureties.

Samuel Zucker [fig. 9.], alias Edward Von Dalwick, Baron Jules Mercy and Camillon, another con artist, aged 18 in 1903, was 5 ft. 7 inches tall, with black hair, dark brown eyes, of sallow complexion, medium build, and with good teeth. The latter was an important part of the con artist's equipment, especially if the likely victims were women. The bowler hat, starched collar and waistcoat were all part of the con artist's uniform. The only blemish was a mole on the right side of his chin. There were two offences on his known record, at an interval of ten years, suggesting that this was simply the tip of the iceberg. In 1903, he was convicted for false pretences before Bath Quarter Sessions, receiving a sentence of 4 months in prison. In 1913, he committed the same offence and was convicted at Bradford Quarter Sessions, receiving a sentence of 9 months. Zucker, as his name implied was probably Swiss or German, and posed as a continental aristocrat as part of his method of relieving people of their money or jewellery.

J. Bassett [fig. 10.], alias Freckett, Foster, Vincent, Harris, Walter, aged 26, had travelled widely during a long, criminal career extending from 1891 to 1913. He was 5 ft. 8 inches, with brown hair, grey eyes, a fair complexion, of medium build, and with the indispensable good teeth. Slightly marring his handsome appearance were the scars on each eyebrow and another on his forehead. What is extraordinary is the geographical range of his criminal activities, beginning in Rochester, through Tralee, Dublin and Cork in Ireland, Berwick, Northampton, Reading, Stafford, Wakefield and finally at the Taunton Assizes. All the cases were larceny and false pretences and sentences rose from 3 months with hard labour to 5 years penal servitude. Clearly, the more sophisticated the criminal, the more mobile they were, not only in Britain, but including some from abroad.

fig 10: Portrait of J. Bassett, undated. A much travelled con artist with a long criminal career.
Bath Record Office, Bath & North East Somerset Council

Conclusion

Studying the faces in these and many other criminal portraits of the time has its own, intrinsic fascination. In the great majority of cases, faces do not reveal criminal tendencies as Victorians believed. They do reveal a capacity for artful disguise and deliberate deception and all too often show the ravages of drink and the toll of terms of imprisonment served with hard labour. Then as now, the prison system may have succeeded in locking people away from the public, but signally failed in deterring criminals from committing future crimes. The pattern of crimes in Bath was, at least in part, determined by its social structure. The common presence of beggars, some of whom feigned disability, reflected the strength of charities in Bath and the willingness of the clergy and ladies to donate money to them. The tradition is continued with the present-day buskers who are all too evident in the central streets of Bath. Crime among female domestic servants reflected the presence of the servant-keeping classes who lived in the big houses in the city, prominent among them were elderly widows living in Lansdown and Bathwick. The presence of the latter was also an attraction for professional con artists who made their way to Bath from other parts of the country and abroad, looking for unlawful gains from wealthy widows who might fall prey to the flattery and attention from handsome, well-dressed young men. Again, a certain historical continuity suggests itself. In Georgian Bath, rakes and fortune hunters made their way to the city in search of heiresses and the 'swell mob' sought criminal opportunities as card sharps or pickpockets. In Victorian and Edwardian Bath, the con artists came in search of rich pickings, an appropriate form of crime for a city that prided itself on its genteel image.[29]

Notes

1. Donald Thomas, *The Victorian Underworld* (London, 2000), p.1.
2. *History of Surveillance*, Part 1, Channel 4 television series, 2001.
3. The first modern force was the Irish county police system founded in 1787.
4. Stanley H. Palmer, *Police and Protest in England and Ireland 1780-1850* (Cambridge, 1988), pp.435-57.
5. See the evidence of M.D.Hill, Parliamentary Papers, 1852, vii, Report of the Select Committee on Criminal and Destitute Juveniles, Minutes of Evidence.
6. Edwin Chadwick, *The Sanitary Condition of the Labouring Population of Great Britain*, 1842, rep. 1965.

7. Henry Mayhew, *London Labour and the London Poor* (London, 1861).
8. L. Perry Curtis Jr., *Apes and Angels: The Irishman in Victorian Caricature* (rev. ed. Washington and London, 1997), chapter 1, Physiognomy, pp. 1-15.
9. L. Perry Curtis Jr., *Apes and Angels.*
10. Frankie Morris, *Artist of Wonderland: The Life, Political Cartoons, and Illustrations of Tenniel* (Cambridge, 2005).
11. Fussleton Letters, Letter VIII, From Sir Hector Stormer to Admiral Tornado, Bath Pamphlets, Vol. 40. Bath Central Library.
12. Fussleton Letters, Letter IV, Will Fussleton Esq., to J.O. Esq., Feb. 1836. Capt. Carroll, R.N., became the first Chief Constable of the Bath Police in 1836.
13. J.J. Tobias, *Crime and Industrial Society in the 19th century* (Batsford, 1967), p.140.
14. *The Bath Chronicle,* April 26th 1849.
15. *The Bath Chronicle,* July 7th 1864.
16. Reports of the Chief Constable, 1885-1894, include annual totals of tramps and vagrants conveyed to the Casual Ward of the Workhouse. The figures suggest a rising trend in the 1880s and 1890s: 1885 – 4,675; 1886 – 4,624; 1887 – 5,074; 1888 – 5,853; 1889 – 6,204; 1891 – 4,578; 1892 – 5,633; 1893 – 7,727; 1894 – 9,577.
17. There is a gap between the number of offences known to the Police and the actual level of crimes committed because not all crimes are reported to the Police, especially cases of personal assault and rape cases. Comparing the number of offences recorded over time can be distorted by changes in legislation, so creating new crimes, and by a crackdown on certain offences such as begging or vagrancy at the whim of the Chief Constable.
18. *The Bath Chronicle,* September 13th 1849.
19. See Memorial to the Watch Committee, 1865 on the closing of public houses at 1 am. Bath Record Office.
20. Tobias, *Crime and Industrial Society in the 19th century,* pp. 122-147.
21. Report of the Chaplain, W.C.Osborne, Bath City Gaol, 1849, Bath Record Office.
22. Reports of the Chief Constable.
23. *The Bath Chronicle,* October 12th 1848.
24. Reports of the Chief Constable.
25. For instance, there were 139 lodgers recorded in the census for Avon Street in 1871. Census Enumerator's schedules, Walcot Parish, Bath.
26. A.E. Dingle, 'Drink and Working Class Living Standards in Britain, 1870-1914', *Economic History Review,* 1972, pp. 608-622.
27. Post Office Directory, Bath, 1860-1 and 1900.
28. I would like to acknowledge the help given me by Sergeant Bob Allard of the Bath Police in accessing the records. They are now held in Bath Record Office.
29. Graham Davis and Penny Bonsall, *A History of Bath: Image and Reality* (Lancaster, 2006).

Public Housing in Bath, 1890-1925

Malcolm Hitchcock

Introduction

In response to both national legislation and local need, Bath City Council has for more than a century provided, maintained and administered a large proportion of the housing stock within the city.[1] This study sets out the story of the provision of purpose-built municipal housing in Bath, and covers the period from the late 1890's to a time of major change at the end of the First World War and the early 1920's.

§

National Legislation and Acts of Parliament.

Several items of major legislation were passed in the second half of the nineteenth century aimed at alleviating the twin evils of poor public health and acute poverty, it being well understood that the common factor that linked them was inadequate housing. There is not space here to go through all the bills in detail, but rather to consider the two cornerstone nineteenth-century Acts of Parliament that have had an enduring effect on public health, and launched the programme of Council House building throughout the nation.

The Magna Carta of public health, the Parliamentary Act of 1875, introduced a code of sanitary law, covering the supply of wholesome water and sewage removal, housing standards, regulation of the streets, control of epidemic diseases, and burial of the dead. It remained on the statute book for the next sixty years, and immediately gave rise to model byelaws regarding aspects of town planning to be drawn up to provide guidance to local authorities.[2] Thus byelaw housing, privately funded terraces in tightly packed patterns, were built at most city perimeters. These late-Victorian terraces are still to be seen in every large town.[3] The Act also enhanced the powers of the local Medical Officer of Health, one of whose functions was to notify the council

Facing: Detail of first public houses built in the Dolemeads, c.1906
The houses on the left were elevated for protection from the persistent risk of flooding.
Bath in Time – Bath Central Library Collection

when the standards set out in the act were not being observed.

In 1890, the Housing of the Working Classes Act placed a duty on local authorities, having given them sufficient powers, to demolish inadequate housing and to replace it with new. This Act stretched to sixty pages, repealed fifteen previous acts, and its main thrust was as follows-

> 'where it appears to the Local Authority that the closeness, narrowness, bad arrangement or bad condition of any buildings, or the want of light, air, ventilation or proper conveniences, or any sanitary defect in any buildings are dangerous or prejudicial to the health of the inhabitants, either of the buildings themselves or neighbouring buildings, and that demolition or reconstruction is necessary to remedy the above evils it is the duty of the Sanitary Authority to act by passing a resolution to the above effect and prepare a scheme for the improvement of the area'.[4]

The main provisions were that any houses inspected by the Medical Officer of Health and thereafter declared 'unfit for human habitation' for want of the amenities given above, and if discussions with the owners proved fruitless, these should be compulsorily purchased and demolished and the occupants re-housed. However, the cost would not be borne by central government, but through a local government loan to be repaid by an increase in the local rates. It was this requirement that caused local councils and their planners nationwide to wrestle with the problem of how to provide housing at low cost. Councils did not merely replicate the Victorian tenements that had already degenerated into slums. They charged a rent that was affordable to those re-housed, and asked their fellow ratepayers, who were not affected, to fund a class of people many believed were undeserving of charity or of much sympathy. Compensation was even paid to slum landlords.

§

Bath City Council's response to the legislation at the turn of the century

In response to the 1875 Public Health Act, densely arranged terraces were built speculatively on green field sites on the edge of the city over the next twenty-five years, to meet the needs of the growing artisan population. These were located in South Twerton around Moorland Road, in Larkhall, and in Fairfield above Camden. Whilst these developments alleviated some of the overcrowding in the city centre, they had little impact upon the poorest members of society. The Act reiterated that the office of Medical Officer of Health be set up to provide local authorities with data upon which to act to sustain and improve good community health. Bath's first Medical Officer of Health, Dr.C.S. Barter, had been appointed nine years earlier in 1866, and some of his duties were concerned with his assessment of the housing stock:-

> 5. He will make out a list of houses in which deaths may occur from zymotic (epidemic) diseases with a view to make a special enquiry into their condition as regards drainage, ventilation, cleansing, water supply, etc. and report to the Board as may be needful.
>
> 7. When so many as three deaths occur in any one house in a year, it will form an object for special enquiry and inspection with a report to the Board if it should appear needed. These enquiries will have their first application in the poorer and most densely inhabited districts.[5]

These, and his other duties, such as preparing regular reports, were contained within the Act. Firstly Dr. Barter and thereafter Dr. Anthony Brabazon, Medical Officer of Health from 1876, throughout his twenty-year tenure, prepared monthly and annual reports to the Sanitary Committee. These reports, included statistics on causes of death, categorized by age and district, with brief explanatory notes, as well as data on external factors - national epidemics, weather conditions and flooding. Dr. Brabazon had a long and distinguished career, having served at the Crimea and later as a physician at the Mineral Water Hospital, in addition to his duties as a private practitioner. A memorial window is to be seen in St. Mary's Church, Bathwick, where he served as churchwarden for most of his thirty-five years in the city. He died, still working at the age of 76, and his funeral and achievements were reported effusively.[6]

In reading Dr. Brabazon's reports one gets no sense that urgent remedial action needed to be taken to improve the health of Bath's citizens at the end of the century. To paraphrase from a memorandum written by his successor, Dr. Symons, placing Bath in a national context:

> Bath is not now an overcrowded city, as it was in 1851…While the number of houses in the central city parishes remain practically the same, the population has decreased 35%; overcrowding has vanished. The migration to the suburbs has resulted that, according to the Registrar General's return for 1891, 4.1% of the population of Bath were considered to be living in overcrowded tenements as against 11.2%, the English average for town and country.[7]

Dr. Brabazon, by contrast, in his report for 1894, several years after the passing of the Housing of the Working Classes Act, wrote:

> I have endeavoured to carry out with the assistance of the Inspector and the Surveyor the duties imposed upon me under the Act for the Better Housing for the Poor, and at the request of the Sanitary Committee I have personally visited and inspected houses let in tenements in those streets known to me as requiring strict investigation….209 houses were thoroughly inspected. I have seen enough to prove that much can be done to obtain the object of the Act. Were I asked to point out localities where I considered the houses most unfit for healthy human habitation, I would mention… (Here he gives a short list, and hopes that a new project to improve Milk St will be carried out).[8]

This gives the impression that he regarded this Act as not altogether relevant to Bath, and its tenor, involving eviction, compulsory purchase, demolition, re-housing the dispossessed, architects, builders and contracts, implied an effort out of proportion to the scale of the problem. To this must be added the damaging effects on tourism, and increases in local rates. It would not be surprising if a gentleman then in his seventies had wanted little to do with it.

So why did Bath, which advertised itself as a health resort, with few areas of overcrowding, and a good record on public health, become one of the first cities in the country to introduce local authority housing?[9] One answer lies in examination of the personalities of two officials who were intimately concerned with the housing problem.

§

Dr. William Symons and Charles Fortune

Dr. Brabazon's successor in Bath, Dr. William Symons, was appointed in 1896 when aged 42, having held several important posts in London. There the first major national municipal housing scheme had been prepared in 1893 for the London County Council and the dwellings opened by the Prince of Wales in March 1900.[10] This new estate of five-storey tenements at Bethnal Green on a 15-acre site involved the demolition of over 700 houses.[11] Dr. Symons would have been well aware of this programme to provide decent housing for the poor and, furthermore, he maintained contacts with influential colleagues from which he often derived support during his career in Bath. He was a forceful character who was determined to bring about change, and as *The Bath Chronicle* in his obituary pointedly wrote, 'soon after his election it became evident that developments were to be expected.'[12] This caused unease among some members of the Sanitary Committee, and led to complaints that the new MOH was 'expensive and extravagant'.[13] Immediately, he concerned himself with the housing issue, and by comparing their reports on Lampard's Buildings, one can contrast the approach towards the condition of slum dwellings from their views on one of its courts:

> Viners Court is improperly termed a Court being a wide open space containing 11 two storey houses, generally having three rooms, one on the ground floor and two above. The drainage is outside the houses - there are 6 W.C.s and a tap for a separate water supply. The houses in this Court, as in the others, labour from a very serious defect - the want of through ventilation; they are exactly in this respect under the circumstances as back-to-back houses and thus cannot be pronounced to be in accordance with the Laws of Sanitation. Here again I would advise the Committee to give instructions to ascertain what steps can be taken towards improving or rather removing this insanitary

condition. In many of these houses there are structural defects, on which the Surveyor's opinion would be valuable.[14]

To refer more particularly to ten of the cottages in Viner's Court (excluding No. 7). These were originally 2-roomed, but the upper has been divided in two by a wooden partition; the smaller has a capacity of about 370 cubic feet, and is very badly ventilated, and open space from 7 to 15 inches in height over the door providing the double purpose of illumination and ventilation. In such cabins as this two or three children sleep in six of the cottages. As regards water supply, one tap provides the wants of 54 persons. The W C's are in the front garden, one being common to two houses, are fully exposed to view and are difficult to access by night or in bad weather. This leads to the retention of excrement in vessels in rooms, which are otherwise filthy. The three rooms are connected directly one with another, so there is one atmosphere, and a sickly odour pervades the dwelling. The walls of the cottages are in my opinion dangerous; a small plot of garden gives an air of comfort, and has probably saved them from earlier demolition. All this within a stone's throw of some of the best property in Bath. As a result of my inspection I feel justified in representing the Lampard's Building Courts… to be a unhealthy area within the meaning of the Housing of the Working Classes Act, 1890.[15]

Dr. Brabazon's assessment indicates that their situation was not beyond repair; Dr. Symons' opinion six years later, was that the situation had not improved and hence the full powers given under the Act should be applied. Dr. Symons carried out an appraisal and his conclusions are contained in his memorandum which set out the state of housing for the local urban poor. Whilst the city's overall population density was well below the national average, it was very unevenly distributed. For example, there were 7.4 persons per acre living in Bathwick, compared with ten times that number in the central parishes. The M.O.H. quoted the 1891 Census, which included details of overcrowding for the first time, showing that there were over three thousand people living as families of three or more in tenements of one or two rooms, and thirty nine families living four, five or six in one room only.

The M.O.H. identified three areas of particular deprivation - Milk Street, (patched up from time to time, but no radical action taken), the Dolemeads, (prone to regular flooding), and Lampard's Buildings above Julian Road, (identified as early as the 1840's as the location of the highest mortality rates in Bath). Thus, in 1896, the Council when faced with the twin pressures from the Acts and periodic reports from the new Medical Officer that many of the properties in the latter two areas were unfit for human habitation, sanctioned the preparation of two schemes to provide municipal housing.

Bath Council was fortunate in employing Charles Fortune as city surveyor from 1888 until his death in 1915, a man who 'did immense work in connection with the undertakings that have had far-reaching effect in our city'.[16] The surveyor was responsible for drawing up plans for all new public authority schemes, for example road widening, new sewerage systems, refuse collection and disposal, electric street lighting, demolition of unsafe houses, and new roads as the city expanded. However, he always described the work he did on public housing, in particular the Dolemeads, as his 'Magnum Opus'. His superb drawings now in the Bath Record Office, of the Dolemeads and Lampard's Buildings, testify to the imagination and care he took in providing houses with between one to four bedrooms to meet a range of accommodation needs. Another project worthy of mention, but not carried out until his death, was the elimination of sewage entering the Avon upstream of central Bath, by piping it directly to the Treatment Works. He was described as one of the 'strong men' of the city, conscientious, indefatigable, robust and plain spoken in pursuance of getting his own way.[17] He and Dr. Symons would have been a formidable pair on the issue of social housing provision.

§

The Scheme for Lampard's Buildings

In response to the Sanitary Committee's instruction, Charles Fortune prepared a scheme that required compulsory purchase and demolition of all the cottages on the eastern side of the street, most of which had been shoddily built on the gardens of houses in Morford Street. These, together with commercial properties such as a brewery (another haven for rodents), were to be replaced by a terrace rising up the slope to Mount Pleasant at the top, the land contours requiring that the basic house designs be adapted to fit in the space. New dwellings were also scheduled for the other side at the junction with Mount Pleasant. [**fig. 1**]. It took four years for the necessary orders, eviction notices and appeals to be dealt with, such that thirty six houses were erected from 1905 at a cost of £13,500 - nearly half of which was the expense of purchase of existing properties and clearing the site.

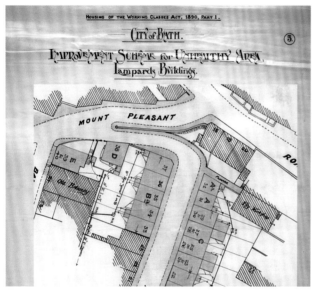

fig 1: Detail from Improvement Scheme for Unhealthy Area, Lampards Buildings, 1899. Part of the site plan, showing building types A, B, C, D and E.
Bath Record Office, Bath & North East Somerset Council

The dwellings themselves were two-storeyed terraced houses of 15-foot frontage. Type A had two and Type B three bedrooms. There were also four double tenement one-bedroom designs one above the other and with separate entrances (Type C) and two four-bedroomed houses (Type D) on Mount Pleasant. The ground floor two-room layout comprised a living room and a scullery/kitchen equipped with a sink and a washing boiler (separately vented to prevent vapour entering the room), and the pantry and coalhouse located under the stairs. The WC was outside as a lean-to extension. Upstairs there were two or three bedrooms in most dwellings.. The one-bedroom maisonettes were similarly equipped. All rooms had fireplaces, with a range in the scullery for cooking, and gas provided illumination. None of the houses had a bathroom, and drawings of the internal room arrangements for the three-bedroomed houses are shown as [**fig. 2**].

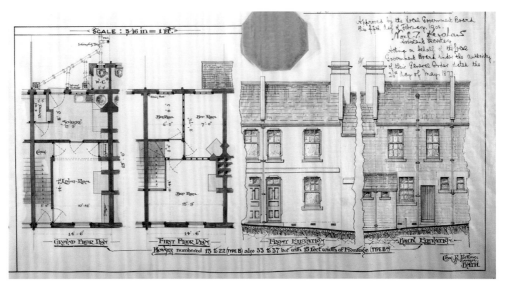

fig 2: Detail showing Plans and Elevations of 3 bedroomed type B housing, 1902. Double Tenement Houses of 3 rooms each were planned for Lampards Buildings. Approved by the Local Government Board, Feb. 5th 1902.
Bath Record Office, Bath & North East Somerset Council

It was calculated that the site would accommodate 176 people, always assuming that two people occupied each bedroom. The drawings bear the stamp and seal of approval from the Local Government Board, to whom all applications had to be addressed. A photograph of the street taken before all properties were demolished in 1970 to make way for the Ballance Street housing scheme is shown as [**fig. 3**].

The Dolemeads Scheme

The Surveyor prepared a scheme for the Dolemeads to build municipally-funded houses after slum clearance which covered a much bigger area, some seven acres, to be cleared in stages as finance would allow. The first phase was finally approved in early 1900; a further three phases followed this, such that it took forty years to reach the northern extremity of Ferry Lane. Flooding of the lower town by the river Avon in the nineteenth century and the devastation caused was a perennial problem,[18] and Fortune included a basic requirement

fig 3: The Ballance Street redevelopment site, July 1970. The neat row of Lampards Buildings still stands, shortly before their demolition as part of the Lansdown Clearance.
Bath in Time – Bath Central Library Collection

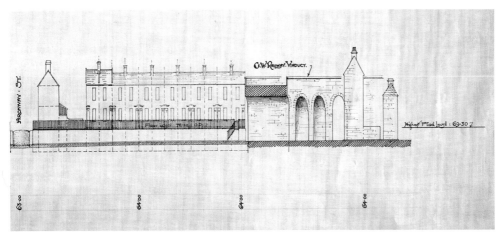

fig 4: Dolemeads Housing & Improvement Scheme, 1906. This section along Middle Lane shows the housing raised to be above the highest indicated flood level.
Bath Record Office, Bath & North East Somerset Council

that the new houses would have their ground floors nearly one foot above the highest recorded flood level of the river. To accomplish this, massive foundations were provided for the houses and 13,000 loads of infill material were imported into the area in the first phase to raise ground level by some thirteen feet. A drawing showing the groundworks is shown as **[fig. 4]**.

In the first phase, ground was cleared and building took place on the relatively open space of about one acre, then occupied by part of Princes Buildings and gardens south of Middle Lane, to allow Excelsior Street and the west side of Archway Street to be constructed. The first of the forty two houses were opened with great ceremony in June 1901 by Dowager Lady Tweedmouth. Her son, Lord Tweedmouth, who as an Alderman on the Housing Committee of the L.C.C. in a speech at the reception afterwards, spoke upon the deprivation in London, where he stated that over 900,000 people were living in contravention of the Public Health Acts. An account from *The Bath Chronicle* of the ceremony and the luncheon afterwards gives a strong impression that Bath was in the vanguard of municipal housing provision.[19] The houses and the opening ceremony are shown as **[fig. 5]**.

The houses were almost identical in style to those at Lampard's Buildings, two storeyed terraces of fifteen-foot frontage, and identically equipped internally. Most had two-bedrooms, however, four, three-bedroomed dwellings were built at the end-terrace, one storey higher to accommodate two extra bedrooms. The rents were set at 5/- per week for the smallest to 6/6d for the 4-beds – scarcely affordable by the average unskilled labourer. Indeed, Dr. Symons wrote afterwards: 'There will no doubt be a ready demand for them at these rentals; but it is obvious that they will be occupied by the well-to-do artisan classes and cannot be considered as making provision for the very poor.'

The next phase took place just before the Great War, when another 18 houses were constructed to become the final terraces of 'red brick houses'; the eastern side of Archway Street with mini-front gardens to set them back from the road, and another to be built after several existing short terraces had been demolished on Middle Lane. A photograph taken prior to this, **[fig. 6]**, shows the first pair on the left having been built at least ten feet above the roadway, with railings provided to prevent accidental falls and access ramps installed at each end, with Moorfield Place and Poplar Terrace beyond soon to be demolished to make way for the remaining houses planned. This new terrace overlooked cottages, St.George's Place and Plato's Buildings on the other side,

fig 5: The opening of the Dolemeads new housing, July 1901. The 'model dwellings for artisans' erected by the Corporation were opened on Monday, Midsummer's Day 1901.
Bath in Time – Bath Central Library Collection

which themselves were demolished after the First World War and the road widened, raised and renamed Broadway in the third phase of building.

fig 6: Middle Lane (later Broadway), Dolemeads, c.1901. On the corner of St. George's Place and Peto's Buildings, the first new cottages on the left are raised above the muddy flood-affected streets.
Bath in Time – Bath Central Library Collection

fig 7: The New Workman's Dwellings, Dolemeads, 1901. Cheaper brick was chosen rather than Bath stone for these dwellings.
Bath in Time – Bath Central Library Collection

House Construction

The Specification for the houses on the Dolemeads site drawn up by Charles Fortune in his own hand, in Bath Record Office, shows that they were well constructed to a high standard, and that traditional methods and top grade materials were employed throughout. **[fig. 7]**. All building work was put out to tender, and F. W. Toogood (a local firm still in business) selected as the lowest at £10,500. Here brick was chosen rather than Bath stone as it was cheaper. Members of the Housing Committee had visited other sites outside Bath to ascertain building costs at first hand. This was supported by advice given nationally in trade magazines such as *The Builder*. The details and Specification for Lampard's Buildings has been lost; however since this was also Fortune's it is reasonable to assume that the work was to an equally high standard. One difference was that the frontage of Lampard's Buildings was faced with stone to be in keeping with the neighbourhood.

§

Change in Direction at the end of the Great War

Lampard's Buildings was complete by 1912 and the Dolemeads terraces soon afterwards. Thereafter, all plans for future development in Bath were shelved until the end of the Great War. However, the attitude towards housing provision was about to change, since during the early years of the twentieth century, British town planners and industrial philanthropists had concluded that the expansions involving high density identical terraces in the previous century had been an error. Whilst they met the physical requirements of the population, they did little for their spiritual needs. One the most influential advocates of change was Raymond Unwin, who having studied model towns at home and abroad, advocated low density layouts of varied design in a semi-rural environment.[20] He stressed the importance of the land contours, open spaces, of aspect with respect to the sun, and provided patterns of properties to deal with specific issues, for example road junctions and access roads. This philosophy led to the concept of the Garden City, and were put into practice for the first time at Letchworth, where a new town was created in conjunction with Barry Parker.[21] Symons and Fortune visited the site during the course of its construction.[22] However, Unwin's book, first published in 1909 and republished immediately after the War was over, did not deal in great depth with actual house design, and so a manual arising out of a Government Enquiry at the end of the War, The Tudor Waters Report, was produced giving a range of designs and floor plans to assist local authorities to put his ideas into practice.[23] One of the designs that was used as a model in Bath is shown in a semi-detached house with three bedrooms that could also be adapted to a short terrace block. **[fig. 8]**.

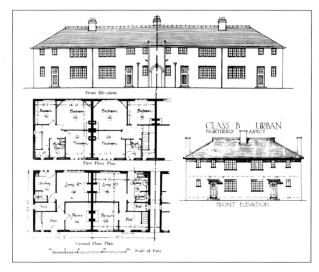

fig 8: **Social Housing Plans 1919.** A three-bedroomed semi-detached house, featured in The Local Government Board Housing Manual on the preparation of State-Aid Housing Schemes.
Bath in Time – Bath Central Library Collection

All this activity would have come to nothing without a national desire to reconstruct the country and give it a better future after the cataclysm of the Great War. The Lloyd George Government set itself the task of eradicating inadequate housing once and for all by building 'Homes fit for Heroes', by passing another great Parliamentary Act, the Housing, Town Planning, &, Act on July 31st 1919 (thereafter known as the Addison Act, after the then Minister of Health). From then on, the Government would fund local authorities by underwriting any losses after deduction of a one penny rate. In return, they would for the first time have a definite obligation to make adequate provision for housing need, and complete the work on time.[24] Bath councillors were left in no doubt that this task was of the highest priority, meeting an urgent need and providing valuable employment for men returning from the front. They appointed a professional architect, A.J. Taylor, to undertake the design, and a full-time Housing Officer in 1921, and bought 25 acres of land between

Englishcombe Lane and the Somerset & Dorset railway, adjacent to the allotment land they already owned. Then they resolved to increase this to 40 acres at a meeting in September, and there to erect 230 houses for those displaced from Little Corn Street after demolition. A proposal to extend the city boundary, to encompass Twerton and also expand towards Weston, was passed in 1925 to provide for future housing development. Also, it was agreed to proceed with the next phase in the Dolemeads, clearing the remaining houses and thereafter building on the other side of Middle Lane.

§

Englishcombe Lane, the first semi-detached houses

The architect's site layout for the Englishcombe Lane estate is shown as [fig. 9], and one can immediately see a radical change of approach. Coronation Avenue, the last of the Victorian-style terraces, was built at a density of 40 houses per acre between 1902 and 1909. These houses strode uncompromisingly in a straight line up the steep slope, soon set beside a community of semi-detached dwellings at 12 houses per acre in a flattened oval pattern broadly running along the contour, with a large green space at the centre and small closes leading off it. This was Bath's first garden suburb - the rural nature emphasised

fig 9: Site layout for the Englishcombe Estate, 1920. Bath's first Garden Suburb, all the closes were given arboreal names.
Bath Record Office, Bath & North East Somerset Council

in that all the closes were given arboreal names. The house designs owed a great deal to the Manual; they were to be three-bedroomed, and the downstairs rooms were reversed when necessary to ensure that the living room received the sun, regardless of which side of the street they were placed. The bathroom and separate toilet were upstairs. The Manual suggested two styles of downstairs living quarters should be built; some should have a living room and a separate smaller parlour, and for others (110 houses in all at Englishcombe), the parlour was dispensed with and the kitchen enlarged. In this case a lower rent was charged. A drawing of one of these houses is shown as **[fig. 10]**.

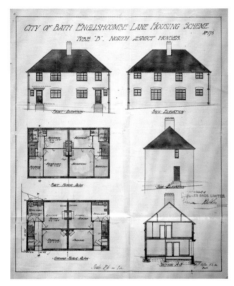

fig 10: City of Bath Englishcombe Lane Housing Scheme, undated. Type 'B' three-bedroomed north aspect houses designed by Alfred J. Taylor, architect.
Bath Record Office, Bath & North East Somerset Council

fig 11: Aerial view of the Englishcombe Estate, 12th April 1947. This post-war aerial survey shows the development, completed at the end of 1925.
English Heritage – National Monuments Record

The exterior walls were built of Bath stone, and again, the best materials were used. The houses were fitted with gas only, after cost estimates had been received from both gas and electricity companies,[25] and this caused endless trouble in later years, with petitions being received in 1934 from disgruntled residents demanding an electricity supply. A road constructed through the allotments down the line of the Monksdale Brook connected the estate directly with the lower town,[26] and eight Bath-based building contractors, in order to give the maximum amount of local employment, were commissioned to build the first batch of 42 houses in the summer of 1920. Work continued through the following years, with allocations of 50 houses being released periodically, such that the estate was complete by the end of 1925. An aerial photograph showing its final appearance is shown in [fig. 11].

§

Concluding Remarks

Many more estates were to be provided by Bath City Council over the next twenty-five years. Throughout that period, the principles laid down at Englishcombe – low density plus open space, good quality materials, and sympathy with the environment - were always observed. The story of public housing in Bath has its unsung heroes in the figures of Dr. Symons and C.R. Fortune. Bath was fortunate in having local officials of real calibre in the pioneering developments in public housing. Their contribution to the implementation of subsidised housing, part of a truly significant, national movement, was to transform the living conditions of thousands of Bath citizens during the twentieth century. Today, problems with the supply of affordable housing remain unresolved and a few councils are now looking at a modest return to council houses as a solution.

Notes

1. Somer Community Housing Trust took over the provision of Municipal Housing in 1999 and currently administers over 9,500 dwellings, most of which are in Bath, and only 10% of which are Georgian or Victorian town houses which pre-date this study.
2. Local Government Board, *Local Byelaws for the use of Sanitary Authorities. IV New Streets and Buildings,* 1877.
3. Stefan Muthesius, *The English Terraced House* (Yale, 1982).
4. The Housing of the Working Classes Act, 1890.
5. Bath Corporation Minute Book, *Medical Officer of Health. Statement of Duties as defined by the Town Council.* Jan. 1866. Bath Record Office.

6. 'Death of Dr.Brabazon', *The Bath Chronicle*, March 19th, 1896.

7. W.M. Symons, M.O.H. for Bath, *The Housing of the Working Classes*, 1900.

8. Dr. Brabazon, Annual Report of the Medical Officer of Health, 1891. Bath Record Office.

9. Statistics for the last ten years of the century showed that death rates caused by three groups of diseases associated with inadequate living conditions - zymotic infections during childhood, tubercular, and bronchial/pneumonia were 60 per cent, 80 per cent and 80 per cent respectively of the national average for England and Wales. 'Dr.W.M. Symons; Founder of Bath's Health Department. Obituary', *The Bath Chronicle*, March 19th 1916.

10. 'Boundary-Street Buildings, Bethnal Green', *The Builder*, March 10th 1900, p.237.

11. For a description of the evolution of this estate, some of which has now been demolished, refer to Bridget Cherry and Nikolaus Pevsner. *The Buildings of England London 4 North*, (1998) p.587.

12. 'Dr. W.M. Symons, Founder of Bath's Health Department. Obituary', *The Bath Chronicle*, March 19th 1916.

13. He had many other interests beside the link between housing and well-being, as can be seen in his Annual Report to the Sanitary Committee, transforming it from three or four pages of copperplate handwriting by Dr. Brabazon into a typed document of some 50 pages crammed with statistics and other data covering all aspects having an impact on public health.

14. Dr. Brabazon, M.O.H. Report, April 1892.

15. Dr. Symons, M.O.H. Report, October 1898.

16. 'C.R. Fortune. A Man of Energy and Efficiency. Obituary', *The Bath Chronicle*, October 30th 1915.

17. C.R. Fortune, Obituary.

18. R.A. Buchanan, 'The Floods of Bath', *Bath History* Vol. VII, p.167.

19. 'Workman's Dwellings in the Dolmeads. Report of the Opening Ceremony', .*The Bath Chronicle* , June 24th 1901.

20. Raymond Unwin . *Planning in Practice*. 1909, revised 1919.

21. A description of this movement is to be found in Arthur Evans, *The Design of Suburbia* (1982), and its application to Bath in Christopher Pound, *The Genius of Bath* (1986).

22. Dr. Symons and Charles Fortune visited the new town of Letchworth in Hertfordshire in October 1905. Although they found the overall planning of the site good, and some of the fittings ingenious, particularly the kitchen range and bath, they considered the building standards inferior to those in Bath, with an absence of durability and finish. They considered the overall concept was not applicable to Bath, as it required large areas of cheap land.

23. Local Government Board, *Manual on the Preparation of State-Aided Housing Schemes*. HMSO, 1919. This document emphasized in its Introduction the pressing urgency of the need to provide new homes: 'The Government and the Country are looking to Local Authorities to start at once on schemes rightly regarded as forming the most urgent part of the Restructuring Programme'.

24. In a Report from the Bath Town Clerk to the Housing Committee, Feb. 1921, he stated that Dr Addison estimated that approximately 200,000 houses per annum would be needed nationally over the next few years. The latest returns showed that contracts had been executed between Local Authorities and builders for 145,000, and he was concerned as to whether there were sufficient resources to sustain such a programme, both nationally, but more particularly in Bath itself. This then caused much soul-searching amongst councillors who would then have to find £500,000, the estimated Government subsidy, if the first post-war programme could not be completed in time. The strict timescales were relaxed later, the estate taking over four years to complete.

25. Local Government Board, *Manual on the Preparation of State-Aided Housing Schemes*. HMSO, 1919. The figures were, for installation per house:- Gas only lighting, and water heating to geyser, copper and cooker £43. Lighting by electricity and hot water circulation from range £97. Dual system- electric light and gas water heating £69. Gas was selected, subject to Ministry of Health approval.

26. This land had been purchased ten years earlier to install municipal allotments in response to The Small Holdings and Allotments Act, 1908 which placed an obligation on local Authorities to provide for the urban poor. Refer to *Journal of the Survey of Old Bath and District*, Nos 21&22.

Acknowledgements

I wish to thank Colin Johnston in the Bath Record Office for providing Council Minutes and Architect's Drawings, and also invaluable assistance in the production of this article, and also Daniel Brown of Bath in Time at Bath Central Library for permission to reproduce figures 3, 5, 6, 7 and 8 and the National Monuments Record at Swindon for permission to reproduce figure 11.

Yehudi Menuhin and Bath: A mutual benefit?

Tim Bullamore

Yehudi Menuhin was artistic director of the Bath Festival from 1959 to 1968 – ten festivals, during which time the world beyond Bath was undergoing a dramatic cultural revolution. At the outset of his tenure his was already a household name. By the time he left he was a distinguished elder statesman; and he was to remain so until his death thirty-one years later.

The purpose of this paper is to pose the question: who benefited the most from Yehudi Menuhin's association with the city, Menuhin or Bath? It has often been reported that Menuhin put the city on the cultural map. Indeed, some publications have erroneously reported that Menuhin founded the Bath Festival. Recently, one of the glossy magazines that come through our letterboxes spoke of the festival "started by Yehudi Menuhin". Humphrey Burton refers to Bath as 'his', ie, Menuhin's festival.[1] Indeed, even Menuhin, in June 1968, while preparing for his last festival, said: 'I feel I have brought *my* festival to Bath'[2] (author's italics). He certainly did not start the festival, nor did he bring his festival from anywhere else – there was no previous Menuhin festival other than the family gathering in Gstaad in Switzerland where he had made his home since 1957. The premise that he raised the cultural and artistic profile of the city does stand up to scrutiny, but did the city at the same time revive Menuhin's flagging career? Indeed, to undertake a bit of crystal ball gazing, would Menuhin have had much of a future career if he had not spent a decade as director of the Bath Festival? Did the city do him as much good as he did for the city?

The Bath Festival as we know it today came into being in April 1948. It was the brainchild of the impresario Ian Hunter (later Sir Ian Hunter) and was at first called the Bath Assembly. Its initial aim was to be a festival of the arts for young people. True to those intentions the opening concert of that first Assembly was also the first public performance by the National Youth Orchestra. Running the Bath Assembly was by no means a full-time job for an ambitious young impresario. Indeed, Hunter was considered to be such an upstart that he was removed after the first festival. The city tried to run the festival itself, but in 1955 had to return to Hunter on bended knee and ask him to come back.

Facing: fig 1: Yehudi Menuhin takes rehearsal in the Guildhall, 1962   139
Memorably photographed sitting in the lotus position, Yehudi Menuhin
directs with the bow of his violin.
Photograph – Axel Poignant

In the meantime, by way of historical note, we should be aware that Menuhin had taken part in the 1952 Festival – programmed by a council officer.[3] He was at this stage thirty-six years old and had just returned from a series of ten concerts in February and March in India, where he had been invited by Prime Minister Nehru,[4] and would later visit Israel, where there were still some highly charged feelings over his musical collaboration with the German conductor Furtwängler immediately after the Second World War. In that 1952 concert in Bath, which took place on May 28th, Menuhin gave a recital at the Forum accompanied by his brother-in-law, Louis Kentner. A publication called *The Bath Critic* wrote: 'If this concert had consisted simply of the movement from the Kreutzer Sonata which was given as a third encore, the audience would have had their money's worth.'[5] But even after this, the fifth festival, the city fathers were already squabbling about money. The city had offered a guarantee against loss of £1,000. The loss was in fact almost £1,300.

Alas, bureaucrats are not great impresarios. As already mentioned, in 1955, in desperation at the monotony of its festival, the city swallowed its pride and asked Hunter to return to run the festival. That year Menuhin gave three concerts in the festival. One was a duo recital at the Guildhall with the violinist Gioconda de Vita, which included some wonderfully obscure classics such as a pair of duets by Viotti and Spohr's Duo for Two Violins. Another was Viotti's Violin Concerto No. 22 with the Royal Philharmonic Orchestra conducted by Sir Thomas Beecham. It must have been a small orchestra, as the concert took place within the confines of the Guildhall. The third was an unaccompanied recital in Bath Abbey of music by Bach. Based on the reviews for this and previous concerts, my discussions with Menuhin, and talking to people associated with the festival at that time, I believe that this concert, four years before he even became artistic director, was arguably the high point of Menuhin's violin playing career in Bath. Morley Pooley, *The Bath Chronicle*'s music critic, wrote:

> 'A solitary figure, clutching a violin, stood in front of the choir stalls in Bath Abbey on Tuesday evening, and paused while the huge crowd of people who had flocked to see him settled quietly in their seats. Behind him the newly-restored East Window stood out in bold relief like a beacon of faith, before him a sea of upturned faces waited expectantly. And as he drew his bow across the strings of his fiddle, magic seemed to fill the air. For

ninety minutes he played almost continuously, and throughout that time there was scarce a rustle to break the spell he wove. The player was Yehudi Menuhin, probably the greatest violinist alive today; the instrument he held – almost as old as parts of the beautifully proportioned Abbey Church which formed such a wonderful background to the music of the greatest of all writers of church music, Johann Sebastian Bach – was a priceless Strad.'[6]

fig 2: Yehudi Menuhin, 1961. Pictured during the Bath Festival of 1961
Bath in Time – Bath Central Library Collection

It is perhaps worth pausing at that moment in 1955 to consider the point that Menuhin's career had reached. Yehudi Menuhin was born in New York on April 22nd 1916 to Ukrainian-Jewish immigrants[7], Moshe and Marutha. He was named Yehudi – which literally means Jew – to make a statement to his parents' anti-Semitic landlady. The family moved to San Francisco where, at the age of seven, Yehudi gave his first public recital. Soon he gave a performance of the Mendelssohn concerto. The one thing all those who heard him agreed about was the purity of his tone and the seeming effortlessness of his technique. All the biographies, including Magidoff, Burton, and the controversial Palmer tale, speak of a somewhat unreal childhood. Tony Palmer in particular was granted an extensive interview with Menuhin's sister, Yaltah. In it she said: "We never knew, until it was much too late, how utterly isolated we were, that we were not living the life of children at all."[8] **[fig.2]**

Before long Menuhin's parents were advancing his career. He was in

Paris at the age of ten, where he met Georges Enesco, the Romanian composer, whom Menuhin persuaded to be his teacher.[9] At this time the kings of the violin would have been Fritz Kreisler and Jascha Hefitz.[10] Moshe Menuhin, Yehudi's father, was enthusiastic. He wrote a letter dated August 29th 1928 to Ibbs & Tillett in London, who at the time managed Rachmaninov, Hofmann, Cortot, Casals and Moiseiwitsch. In it he said: 'We shall take Yehudi to London… There is no reason why Yehudi should not carry London as he carried Paris, and thus sell out the Albert Hall.'[11] Yehudi had not so much as played a note in England at that time. But even then some felt that a little caution was needed in promoting this child prodigy. Ibbs & Tillett – remarkably, with hindsight – turned down the opportunity; instead the agency recommended him to the personal attention of Lionel Powell, a partner in the rival firm of Harold Holt, which Ian Hunter would later join.[12]

Despite this rare rejection, Menuhin's pre-war career in Britain was substantial and is well documented. His British debut was on November 10th 1929 in a performance of the Brahms concerto with the London Symphony Orchestra conducted by Fritz Busch, followed by a recital at the Royal Albert Hall.[13] It was after his Berlin debut that year that Albert Einstein famously remarked: 'Now I know there is a God in heaven.'[14] Later that same year came the first truly emotional demand on Menuhin the man. Four years before the Nazis came to power he was asked by concert organisers in Munich to withdraw music by the Jewish composer Ernest Bloch from his programme. He refused.[15] Hitherto, he had rarely had to deal with difficult issues. As his sister Hephzibah once wrote: 'We were mentally cognisant of every problem, but only as a theoretical dilemma.'[16] His other sister, Yaltah, added: 'Like everything else in our family, we never realised until it was too late that the world was not as we had been led to believe. And so we have to constantly resurrect ourselves like corpses, but now with half our brains gone and our hearts pickled.'[17] Then there came the legendary recording, in 1932, at the age of sixteen, of the Elgar concerto with the seventy-five-year-old composer conducting. It was dreamt up by Fred Gaisberg at His Master's Voice to celebrate the composer's seventy-fifth birthday[18] – but poor old Elgar's contribution has been somewhat overshadowed ever since. Most biographers relate the, slightly exaggerated, tale of how Menuhin arrived from France three days before the recording session to work with the composer. After hearing the first few bars Elgar, supposedly, stopped him and said: 'I can add nothing. It cannot be done better. Let's go to the races.' Menuhin was only sixteen. His mother still dressed him. Apart from his spat with the authorities in Munich, he was very unworldly. The Nazi atrocities, of which he would later witness the aftermath, had yet to occur. Menuhin genuinely believed that music could solve every problem.

Alas, three years later, by the age of nineteen, Menuhin was, in modern parlance, burnt out.[19] In 1935 he gave 110 concerts in sixty-three cities in thirteen countries on four continents – and all of this before the days of air travel. The strain was showing. One of his New York fans, Lydia Perera, noted in her diary: '22 March 1936: Concert in Town Hall. Toscanini in mother's box. Yehudi looks tired and weak. 29 March 1936: Yehudi looks tired, indifferent and sad. I had to grit my teeth as I left the hall to keep from crying.'[20] The child prodigy was gone. Now he needed to become a man. As he later said: 'My technique left me. Suddenly I felt I knew nothing.'[21] Menuhin cancelled all his concerts and withdrew to the family home at Los Gatos in California. According to his obituaries, he spent several years rebuilding his talents. He had to. His early training had, in fact, been severely deficient. He had played by instinct. When he had first auditioned for Ysaÿe in Brussels at the age of seven, he played flawlessly for the old composer. But Ysaÿe said: 'You have made me very happy, little boy, very happy. And now, play an arpeggio, just an ordinary arpeggio in three octaves.' Menuhin struggled with the simple exercise. 'I thought so,' muttered Ysaÿe. 'You will do well Yehudi to work on your scales and arpeggios.' As they left Menuhin turned to his mother and begged: 'Take me to Enesco [the Romanian teacher], please.'[22] Ysaÿe was right. Menuhin had not mastered the underlying techniques of violin playing. He played by instinct. And when he reached adulthood and lost that childhood innocence, he had no solid foundation or training on which to fall back upon. But there were other factors.

As long ago as 1955, Robert Magidoff suggested that his problems were psychological and could be traced to the over-protectiveness of his parents, and in particular his mother who lived until 1998, dying at the age of 100 only 16 months before her son's death.[23] With his mother forever lurking in the background, Menuhin married Nola Nicholas, a lively Australian heiress whose unsheltered background could not have been more different to Menuhin's. The biographies go into great detail of how, almost from day one, she felt stifled, how Menuhin's parents instructed her in how to behave and look after Yehudi, and how, as the marriage deteriorated, Menuhin immersed himself in his music rather than deal with his responsibilities.

Menuhin was very good at spotting publicity opportunities, especially if they could be dressed up as humanitarian work. But on one occasion he bit off more than he could cope with. As soon as the war was over he returned to Germany – a country that he had refused to visit since Hitler came to power in 1933 – to perform for survivors in the death camps, which were now known as displaced persons camps. This precipitated the most serious of his crises. The scenes that he and Benjamin Britten, his accompanist, witnessed in Belsen, where they played twice in a single afternoon, shook Menuhin to his core. The surviving inmates, liberated only a week earlier, had been transferred to the SS barracks because the prison huts had been burnt down. Many were dressed in clothing fashioned from army blankets. Britten was so scarred by what he saw that he only spoke once of the experience. He told Peter Pears how what he and Menuhin had seen had left such a wound that no piece of music that he (Britten) had subsequently written was untouched by the memory.[24] Given that Britten's childhood had been relatively normal, imagine how much greater the shock for Menuhin, seeing the atrocities inflicted on people of his own race. This was the child-like Menuhin, the Peter Pan of music, who was not permitted to cross a road unaccompanied until the age of eighteen and for whom shopping was a preposterous activity to be avoided for ever.[25] Britten, the outcast homosexual who had just written *Peter Grimes*, and Menuhin, the Jewish fiddler; their visit to Belsen was so soon after liberation that no pictures of the atrocity had yet reached a domestic audience. They were totally unprepared for what they encountered. Even forty-five years later Menuhin struggled for words, crying at the memory of the horror of what he had encountered.[26] In his own memoir Menuhin says: 'I shall not forget that afternoon as long as I live.'[27] Menuhin's sister Yaltah once said: 'After Belsen, Yehudi was never the same again. What man would have been? The effect of Nola leaving him, added to what he saw in Belsen, almost destroyed him.'[28] What Menuhin realised was that he had not just witnessed a horror, as in a film or a nightmare, he had witnessed the truth. This was how man was capable of behaving to man. As Tony Palmer wrote: 'If the horror transformed the man, it also knocked the violinist right off balance. And this was a man whose life, indeed the only life he knew, was as a violinist. He was running. He was afraid. And he was not yet thirty years old.'[29] Burton, however, disputes that Menuhin ever saw the true horrors of Belsen, but claims instead that he saw the camp when it had been tidied up.[30]

144

When Menuhin returned to conventional concert halls in the late 1940s critics – and the public – noticed that his playing had lost some of its beauty.[31] Once again, he was having a crisis of technique, this time precipitated by the Belsen experience and the collapse of his marriage. Even the sympathetic Magidoff writes:

'Menuhin grappled with his problems in a wretched kind of isolation. He saw little of his wife, as they became strangers to each other… Shedding habits, especially those automatically acquired and practised for many years, and bringing new habits under conscious control, is as grim an undertaking as any adult could assume.'[32]

This was to become a regular theme: while his playing was filled with emotion, it was often technically flawed. Even Desmond Shawe-Taylor, a mild-mannered critic if ever there was, wrote while reviewing a series of CDs issued in 1991 to mark Menuhin's seventy-fifth birthday: 'Perhaps no violinist of the first order has been so continuously busy as conductor and organiser, or had quite so technically a chequered career.'[33] Nevertheless, the late 1940s and early 1950s saw a busy schedule restored and the dissolution of his first marriage. There was a new, powerful and controlling woman in his life. Menuhin married secondly Diana Gould, a ballerina, on October 19th 1947 at Chelsea Registry Office. Later the same day he gave a concert with the London Symphony Orchestra under George Weldon. Diana, according to Palmer, was determined to put Humpty Dumpty back together again.[34]

There were still difficult times ahead. There were illnesses such as measles and chickenpox, relatively inconsequential in childhood but more serious in adulthood; because of his upbringing Menuhin had been sheltered from them as an infant. There were also the deaths, in aircraft crashes, of the violinists Jacques Thibaut and Ginette Neveu and the pianist William Kapell. These misfortunes led Menuhin to refuse to travel by air for many years to come.[35] The indefatigable Diana – the self-styled 'fiddler's moll' – proved to be defatigable and checked herself into a Swiss clinic for two months suffering from stress.[36] There was also the Magidoff biography in 1956 which, while seeming adulatory today, caused enormous ructions in the Menuhin family.[37] Moshe Menuhin wrote a twelve-page memorandum to his three children denouncing the 'defamation' with which they had cooperated. And then there were the postwar emotions, hard perhaps to envisage today, stirred up by Yehudi's concerts in Germany with the Berlin Philharmonic under Celibidache and later, after his de-Nazification, under Wilhelm Furtwängler. These generated considerable rancour in Israel and the US, so much so that Menuhin was provided with an armed guard in the Jewish state. Although Furtwängler had remained in Germany during the war Menuhin believed that the old conductor had been working against, not for, the regime. A tribunal later agreed. Coming from a man who was not a politician in the conventional sense, this message was extremely powerful. It also endeared Menuhin to Furtwängler more so than perhaps to any other conductor and this bond is arguably heard no better than in their recording in 1947 of the Beethoven Violin Concerto. Still, that pre-war innocence and effortlessness had vanished for ever; the child prodigy was gone. Menuhin now had to work to produce his music. It was no longer a care-free pastime. He found the late 1940s and early 1950s very difficult.

In Bath the festivals of 1956 and 1957 had been cancelled. The 1956 because of an overspend the previous year – the year of the infamous re-enactment of the Battle of Trafalgar on the Recreation Ground that had to be abandoned because of blizzards in May. And the 1957, in which Menuhin had been due to appear with his sister Hephzibah, ostensibly because of petrol rationing.[38] Ian Hunter's 1958 festival was carefully managed from a financial perspective. The absence of a festival since 1955 probably ensured a more favourable reception for the 1958 festivities. After concerts featuring, among others, Yehudi and Hephzibah, Elisabeth Schwarzkopf, Rosalyn Tureck, John Gielgud and Shura Cherkassky, the *Chronicle*'s headline was 'Festival: all pleased'.[39]

On March 5th 1959, Ian Hunter announced that Yehudi Menuhin, now aged forty-two, was to be the artistic director of the Bath Festival for that and subsequent years.[40] By that time both the festival and the violinist had suffered a number of crises. The festival funding was never secure, nor was its political backing. Menuhin was no longer a child prodigy, but he was by no means an elder statesman. In the music industry there is no artist harder to sell than a middle-aged one. Behind his back he was increasingly being mocked for his devotion to the three Ys – yoga, yoghurt and Yehudi.[41] **[fig.1]** His passion for green issues and the child-like innocence of his approach to many difficult questions made him, perhaps, the Prince Charles of his day. So while, with hindsight, we can hail Hunter's move as a masterpiece, it could be that he was solving a problem for his own management company: what to do with Yehudi, his Jewish mama, and Yehudi's new – high-maintenance – wife, Diana. Speaking to the author in 1998 Hunter said: "I was his agent and the great thing with Yehudi was that it kept him interested with new ideas."[42] What a relief for the agent, to have your star artist off your back and interested with new ideas.

There is little doubt that most of the ideas for the festival were Hunter's. Menuhin was the titular head, but he was in no sense running the organisation. He had some say as to who performed at the Bath Festival and what they played, but – coincidentally – many happened to come from Hunter's own roster. In effect, Hunter was being paid to look after the day to day running of the festival *and* receiving ten per cent of the artists' fees. It was a successful business model that Hunter rolled out in several other cities including Edinburgh, Windsor, Brighton and Hong Kong.

For Menuhin the Bath Festival meant that he and his family could stay in one place for more than a couple of nights. **[fig.3]** At the family home in Gstaad, in the Swiss Alps, the Menuhins would rarely spend more than a week together before Yehudi would be off travelling. Even when he was there the family saw little of him. Ten days in the same city were unheard of for the Menuhin circus. In his autobiography Menuhin says: 'To be in charge of a festival is as good as

fig 3: Bath Festival Poster, May 1960. Publicity of the festival arranged with Yehudi Menuhin.
Bath in Time – Bath Central Library Collection

147

a holiday.'[43] Zamira, the daughter from his first marriage who went to live with her father and stepmother when she was twelve, recalled:

> 'Daily life in Gstaad always began with yoga. Which I loathe. My father, in his underwear, standing on his head, and all of us expected to do the same. Then there would be breakfast, and then he'd disappear to practise or dictate letters, or telephone, or chair meetings. Later there would be lunch, and then he'd disappear again. We didn't see that much of him, even in Gstaad.'[44]

A stay of ten consecutive nights at the Lansdown Grove Hotel in Bath was sheer luxury for the Menuhins. Although Yehudi would have four different roles - speaker in a discussion, violinist, viola player and conductor of his own hand-picked chamber orchestra – crucially he did not appear in every event, nor even every day. Compared with his normal schedule, it was relaxing. For the first seven years of the Menuhin era the Festival was billed as 'a festival arranged with Yehudi Menuhin'; from 1966 he was billed as 'artistic director'.[45] In August 1998 he talked about the wide variety of guests who appeared. He said: 'That is what the festival meant to me. Communication and contact with a whole lot of people whom I could invite, who came from every aspect of music making and of human interest.'[46] **[fig. 4]** Indeed, Menuhin's first few years at the Bath Festival saw a stunning array of personalities. On one occasion

fig 4: Yehudi Menuhin rehearses in the Guildhall, 1966.
With familiar portraits looking on, the School's Orchestra rehearse under the chandeliers of the Guildhall.
Bath in Time – Bath Central Library Collection

he wrote to Sir Thomas Beecham: 'I have been entrusted with the Festival at Bath, and with the opportunity of indulging a few of my ambitions.'[47] And the format was pretty much established from 1959: Menuhin's ad hoc orchestra was dubbed the Bath Festival Orchestra, [fig. 5] there were chamber concerts in the Guildhall, flashier events in the Forum, sacred music in the Abbey and token amounts of jazz and music from the Indian subcontinent. In today's era of mass travel and world music concerts, we must not lose sight of just how extraordinary these last events were. A sarod recital by Indian musicians in the Guildhall on June 8th 1959 was unprecedented. And Ravi Shankar's joint

fig 5: Yehudi Menuhin in rehearsal with the Bath Festival Orchestra, 1964. Pictured in the Assembly Rooms. *Photograph – David Farrell*

fig 6: Performers at La Serenissima on a specially constructed pontoon on the river, June 1962. This event was visited by Princess Margaret and Lord Snowdon. The Bath Festival was responsible for many grand and exciting productions. *Bath in Time – Bath Central Library Collection*

concert with Menuhin in 1966 predated the sitar master's collaboration with the Beatles by some months.

By being responsible for – but not taking part in – dozens of concerts Menuhin was in a new position. He could, without trying too hard, take credit for other people's work. He may not have programmed much of the festival, he may not have played in half of it, but it was still Menuhin's festival. As Palmer says, festivals provided him with a musical security that his concert career had of late begun to undermine.[48] And the Bath Festival proved to be a popular affair, both locally and nationally. **[fig. 6]**

The rise in the festival artistically, also brought a rise in popularity of its social side, with events such as a Venetian carnival called La Serenissima, a recreation of the Battle of Agincourt and the notorious Roman Orgy at the Roman Baths in 1961. **[fig. 7]** This latter continued to rankle with Menuhin nearly forty years later. In 1998 he told the author:

> 'I must say I was not particularly pleased about the Roman Orgy. I thought it was a music festival. If we'd gone deeply into the subject and found out what kind of music the Romans were listening to, and followed up the archaeology and the history, that would have interested me enormously. I love frivolity. I love gaiety, I love abandonment, I love improvisation. But to see a lot of rich people get together and find some excuse for getting drunk – that attitude was at odds with my own feeling about it.'[49]

fig 7: The Roman Rendezvous, Great Roman Bath, c.1965. Extremely popular with the participants, less so with Menuhin who deplored the 'Roman Orgy' which became a popular feature of the Bath Festival.
Bath in Time – Bath Central Library Collection

fig 8: Yehudi Menuhin and Nadia Boulanger in discussion at the Guildhall, 1962. The Bath Festival extended out to Wells Cathedral that year where Boulanger conducted Stravinsky's Mass and Menuhin was the soloist in Mozart's Violin Concerto in D major.

Photograph – Axel Poignant

fig 9: Menuhin, Fonteyn and Nureyev onstage at the Theatre Royal, 1964. After a specially choreographed performance of Bartok's Divertimento, one of the highlights of the Bath Festival.
Photograph – David Farrell

Whether because of Hunter or Menuhin or – most likely – the pair of them combining their thoughts and ideas, the Bath festivals of the first half of the 1960s saw some important events including Pears and Britten (1959), Nadia Boulanger conducting (1960) **[fig. 8],** Jacqueline du Pré, aged just sixteen (1961), the London Symphony Orchestra with eighty-seven-year-old Pierre Monteux (1962), a joint concert with Menuhin and Johnny Dankworth (1963), Margot Fonteyn and Rudolf Nureyev (1964) **[fig. 9],** the Smetana Quartet (1965) and Ravi Shankar in a joint concert with Menuhin (1966). But by 1966 times were changing. Menuhin was gradually getting more ambitious. He wanted the festival to change and to move forward – but in his way. Artists' fees and other costs were rising, but the city's grant that year had reached only £3,500. In the 1955 festival it had contributed £5,000. Unease was beginning to mount. The old canard of 'elitism' was being muttered; concerts where black tie was the norm looked increasingly out of place in the Swinging Sixties; the Menuhin entourage seemingly swanned in and swanned out; Menuhin himself was growing irritated with the dilution of the classical music programme. Burton believes the city to be at fault. On the subject of Menuhin being an absentee landlord Burton says that such a criticism 'cannot be sustained: the quality of the programme speaks for itself'.[50] In this Burton fundamentally misses the point: the programme is only part of what makes a festival a festival as opposed to merely a series of concerts or events. In an attempt to mollify Menuhin, the city awarded him the rare honour of the freedom of the city. Although the freedom bought Menuhin's favours for a little longer, arguably it also cemented his role in the Establishment at a time when the world was increasingly disdainful of such rarefied honours. The rot had already set in and granting Menuhin the freedom, far from solving the problems, served simply to exacerbate them.

The 1967 festival got off to a bad start with a storm in a teacup between the Abbey and the festival over who should take part in the festival service. Then, Jacqueline du Pré pulled out of her concert at the last moment to go to Israel to support its troops. Even the ever-supportive Morley Pooley, the long-serving music critic of *The Bath Chronicle* turned ambivalent: 'Basically it is the same formula – the Menuhin family,' he wrote.[51] Something had to change. There would have to be life beyond Menuhin. There was a cosiness – particularly in the insular Menuhin caravan - that sat far too uneasily in the revolutionary fervour of the late 1960s. And Bath, for all its exciting events, never rivalled Salzburg or Edinburgh, nor, says Palmer, did it become an essential place of pilgrimage for the discerning music lover. It never was more than a comfortable bourgeois get-together for the local gentry and their children.[52] Menuhin's answer was to rejuvenate the festival with opera - to be funded by the ratepayers of Bath. The festival board would have been only too well aware of how the city council would react if they approached with a begging bowl. While students were growing long hair and rioting, Bath would like some opera. Burton is highly critical of the local burghers: 'For the philistines who were in the ascendancy in local affairs the festival was becoming too esoteric.'[53]

Menuhin was by now almost as famous for his non-musical work as for his musical work, in particular his humanitarian and mediation work. Within his family, he settled disputes; in his work for Unesco he strove to find solutions to conflict; his work in post-war Germany with the Berlin Philharmonic and Furtwängler helped to draw a line under the Nazi era from a musical perspective. Yet, when it came to the Bath Festival, he could not find a solution. He was adamant that the festival must have opera. And the festival was adamant that it could not afford opera. Menuhin went some of the way, by digging into his own pocket; as a result there were four performances in 1967 of Mozart's *Die Entführung aus dem Serail* produced by Phoenix Opera.[54] Again, accounts vary. Did Menuhin lower his fees, waive his fees or even – as he once claimed - write a cheque for £3,000? We don't know. But as a negotiating stance that perhaps weakened his position.

Who said what to whom, and how exactly Menuhin's tenure was brought to an end, has long since been taken to the grave. There are conflicting accounts, some collected after time has allowed the more raw emotions to subside. Immediately after the 1967 Festival, Morley Pooley wrote in *The Bath Chronicle*: 'In recent years the festival has followed a rather anonymous pattern, with scarcely a distinctive ripple from one June to another to stir the musical waters…' He continued in similar vein, before unveiling a shocking suggestion: 'There is one major change the festival could make. It concerns the artistic director Menuhin himself. Now this, I am aware, may seem like heresy. To the musical world Menuhin is the Bath Festival… Somewhere there has to be found another personality.'[55] The article quickly reached Menuhin, who was in the US. He was suspicious that it had been planted by the festival authorities. There was a sharp exchange of correspondence and, somehow, it was agreed that 1968 would be his tenth and final festival.

To the author's mind Menuhin had simply outstayed his welcome. For the 1968 festival he had prepared and booked a cast for *The Magic Flute*. The festival baulked at the cost and refused to entertain it. In *Unfinished Journey*, Menuhin writes: 'When the town council refused to underwrite a fourth opera, I felt it was my cue to go.'[56] Menuhin's ambitions had moved to a new level; the city had stayed roughly where it was. Menuhin and Bath had outgrown each other. At the time there was a good deal of acrimony and bitterness, some of which spilt over into both the local and the national press. Thirty years later, Menuhin was philosophical about his departure. He said: 'I don't think that directors should remain in their position much more than ten years, because there is always a little sediment.'[57]

The public end of this extraordinary and successful era in the history of the festival came in a peaceful and relaxed way on the last night of the 1968 festival, June 30th. In what was probably the least formal event of his decade-long tenure, Menuhin and the Bath Festival Orchestra gathered at the Assembly Rooms for an evening of Viennese waltzes and polkas. At midnight, no one wanted to leave. For one last time in Bath, Yehudi Menuhin placed his violin beneath his chin. The great virtuoso's final contribution to the Bath Festival was Strauss's *Blue Danube*.[58] [59]

With the Bath Festival Menuhin had enjoyed a platform for ten of the most tumultuous years of the past century. It was a platform that he carefully cultivated. He named his group of musical friends the Bath Festival Orchestra. And when he left he renamed them the Menuhin Orchestra. He recorded with them, and put both his name and the festival's name in record shops the world over. There is no doubt that, artistically and economically, he did a lot of good for Bath; forty years later the city continues to reap the benefits of its association with Yehudi Menuhin. But his presence in the city also did a lot of good for Menuhin. He was no intellectual. He was a genius, an artist, a musician, a statesman and a humanitarian. He called himself, in all seriousness, a 'gypsy'.[60] Even Louis Kentner, his brother in law, wrote as the violinist vacillated between his first wife and his lover (Diana): 'Yehudi may not be a great intellectual luminary.'[61] For the rest of his life, he was the former artistic director of the Bath Festival; there were no more emotional or technical crises other than the infirmities of old age. He had entered the festival as a middle-aged man, and he came out of it as an international treasure, an elder statesman of the world.

Had it not been for the Bath Festival, would there have been a career in the decades after middle-age? It is impossible to know. Without the opportunity to pause each year in the beautiful city of Bath, would his hectic schedule have led to more crises? During all this time Menuhin had also been forging his humanitarian work and developing his school. He went on from Bath to Windsor, where he was director of the Windsor Festival for a mere three years. But there was to be no Windsor Festival Orchestra nor the freedom of the town of Windsor.

Menuhin and Bath, whose need was the greatest? Yes, Bath continues to benefit to this day from its relationship with Menuhin. However, based on the evidence above, it can be argued with some conviction that the career of Yehudi Menuhin, arguably the greatest violinist of the twentieth century, benefited more than has previously been documented from his relationship with the city. **[fig.10]**

fig 10: Souvenir Programme for the Bath Festival, 1963
The festival ran from June 6th to 16th in that year.
Bath in Time – Bath Central Library Collection

Notes

1. Humphrey Burton, *Menuhin* (Faber & Faber, 2000), p.386
2. *The Bath Chronicle*, June 18th 1968
3. Tim Bullamore, *Fifty Festivals* (Mushroom, 1999), p.39
4. Robert Magidoff, *Yehudi Menuhin: the authentic biography* (Robert Hale Ltd, 1956) pp. 256-261
5. *The Bath Critic*, June 1952
6. *The Bath Chronicle*, May 14th 1955
7. Stanley Sadie (ed), *The New Grove Dictionary of Music and Musicians* (MacMillan, 1980) Volume XII, p.167
8. Tony Palmer, *Menuhin: A Family Portrait* (Faber & Faber, 1991), p.25
9. *The Financial Times*, obituary, March 13th 1999
10. *The New York Times*, obituary, March 13th 1999
11. Christopher Fifield, *Ibbs and Tillett: the rise and fall of a musical empire* (Ashgate, 2005), pp.144-146
12. Christopher Fifield, *Ibbs and Tillett: the rise and fall of a musical empire*, p.153
13. Robert Magidoff, *Yehudi Menuhin: the authentic biography*, p.134
14. *The Guardian*, obituary, March 13th 1999
15. Humphrey Burton, *Menuhin*, pp.104-105
16. Tony Palmer, *Menuhin: A Family Portrait*, p.66
17. Tony Palmer, *Menuhin: A Family Portrait*, p.66
18. Humphrey Burton, *Menuhin*, pp.130-133
19. *The Daily Mail*, obituary, March 13th 1999
20. Robert Magidoff, *Yehudi Menuhin: the authentic biography*, p.171
21. *The New York Times*, obituary, March 13th 1999
22. Robert Magidoff, *Yehudi Menuhin: the authentic biography*, p.60
23. Marutha Menuhin, obituary, *The Times*, November 21st 1996
24. Tony Palmer, *Menuhin: A Family Portrait*, p.59
25. Tony Palmer, *Menuhin: A Family Portrait*, p.69
26. Tony Palmer, *Menuhin: A Family Portrait*, p.70
27. Yehudi Menuhin, *Unfinished Journey*, (Methuen, 1976, 1996), p.186
28. Tony Palmer, *Menuhin: A Family Portrait*, p.71
29. Tony Palmer, *Menuhin: A Family Portrait*, p.72
30. Humphrey Burton, *Menuhin*, p.251
31. *The New York Times*, obituary, March 13th 1999
32. Robert Magidoff, *Yehudi Menuhin: the authentic biography*, pp.225-226
33. *The Sunday Times*, April 21st 1991
34. Tony Palmer, *Menuhin: A Family Portrait*, p.76

35.   Humphrey Burton, *Menuhin*, p.342

36.   Humphrey Burton, *Menuhin*, p.341

37.   Humphrey Burton, *Menuhin*, pp.351-353

38.   Tim Bullamore, *Fifty Festivals* (Mushroom, 1999), pp.49-51

39.   *The Bath Chronicle*, June 7th 1958

40.   *The Bath Chronicle*, March 5th 1959

41.   *The Times*, obituary, March 13th 1999

42.   Tim Bullamore, *Fifty Festivals*, pp.53-54

43.   Yehudi Menuhin, *Unfinished Journey*, p.358

44.   Tony Palmer, *Menuhin: A Family Portrait*, p.134

45.   Tim Bullamore, *Fifty Festivals*, p.75

46.   *The Bath Chronicle*, August 19th 1998

47.   Letter to Sir Thomas Beecham dated June 13th 1960; author's private collection

48.   Tony Palmer, *Menuhin: A Family Portrait*, pp.123-124

49.   Tim Bullamore, *Fifty Festivals*, p.62

50.   Humphrey Burton, *Menuhin*, p.389

51.   *The Bath Chronicle*, June 20th 1967

52.   Tony Palmer, *Menuhin: A Family Portrait*, p.125

53.   Humphrey Burton, *Menuhin*, p.388

54.   Tim Bullamore, *Fifty Festivals*, p.79

55.   *The Bath Chronicle*, June 20th 1967

56.   Yehudi Menuhin, *Unfinished Journey*, p.362

57.   Tim Bullamore, *Fifty Festivals*, p.87

58.   Tim Bullamore, *Fifty Festivals*, p.89

59.   Yehudi Menuhin, *Unfinished Journey*, p.362

60.   Humphrey Burton, *Menuhin*, p.506

61.   Humphrey Burton, *Menuhin*, p.268

Other reading:

Diana Menuhin, *Fiddler's Moll* (Weidenfeld & Nicholson, 1984)

Moshe Menuhin, *The Menuhin Saga* (Sidgwick & Jackson, 1984)

Elizabeth Holland

Interview by John Wroughton

Introduction

I first met Elizabeth in the early 1970s. It did not take long for me to become aware of a quick and lively mind, which delighted in precise detail and was exhilarated by discovery. Since then she has given enormous support to my own research, directing me to crucial documents, identifying specific sites within the Stuart city and (through her Chapman genealogy) untangling the complex interrelationships of leading members of the City Council during the period of Civil War, when many families (including the Chapmans) were divided in their loyalty. Generous almost to a fault, she has placed the enormous riches of her research - garnered through countless hours spent in the Bath Record Office - at the disposal of local historians. Many have drawn on this expertise over the years; most have gratefully acknowledged their debt.

Elizabeth, a highly cultured person, is also a true scholar. Painstaking in her search for evidence, she never advocates a theory until it can be fully substantiated. Unsurprisingly, therefore, she is intolerant of sloppy research or half-baked ideas - and is always forthright in expressing her opinion! A formidable opponent when roused, she is nevertheless a loyal and trustworthy friend.

Although she recently gave an impressive interview on television, Elizabeth is by nature both modest and self-effacing. Her public utterances have therefore been infrequent, but her contribution to the understanding of Bath's history has been immense. A prolific writer, she has laid bare the old city in all its former glory and has provided for posterity a wealth of detailed material. Our debt to her is immeasurable.

§

The Interview

JPW: *First of all, Elizabeth, tell us something about your early years and your education.*

Facing: fig 4: Elizabeth at High Littleton, c.1950
Private Collection

EAH: I was born in Farnborough, Hampshire. At the age of around six months, I was taken out to India where my father, J.C.F. Holland (Royal Engineer), had transferred to the Bengal Sappers and Miners. (My father was born in Cawnpore and - when he died - he was, like my mother, legally Indian.) At first we lived at Roorkee, Bengal (now Bangladesh). One of my earliest memories is of a monkey sitting on the veranda by my cot, holding the bars and looking down at me. **[fig.1]** My father was then moved to Quetta in the United Provinces (now Pakistan) to attend a course at the Staff College. Auchinleck (later Field- Marshal) was a lecturer there at the time. We were caught up in an

fig 1: Elizabeth and her brother Charles with two of the staff in India, c.1930
Private Collection

160

early forerunner of the Quetta earthquake, and slept in a tent for a time in case it recurred.

I had my fifth birthday at the time of our return. As we sailed through the Mediterranean, the troops all unwound the binding of their topees and trailed them in the sea. I remember the porpoises accompanying us, presumably also in the Mediterranean. On our return to England, my father was stationed at Larkhill on Salisbury Plain, where he took a signals course. Stonehenge was then a monument on an empty plain with no visitors - just sheep. My father later commuted from Farnborough to the War Office in London, where staff were engaged in research into weapons, better tanks, armoured personnel carriers, guerilla warfare and so on.

My father's frequent postings with the army and our later stay in Canada meant that I went to eight different schools in all. The best was Queen Anne's School in Caversham, near Reading, where I boarded. There was a cricket match, and I was standing in the field thinking what a wonderful school it was. Afterwards we all walked home across the playing fields to tea, including Alison Macdonald (Hannay), the first person to pay a subscription to the Friends of the Survey of Old Bath. It was a blazing hot day, with rooks in the elms. Then suddenly it was Dunkirk, and because the school was in the south, many of the pupils scattered.

fig 2: Elizabeth skating in Winnipeg, 1940
Private Collection

fig 3: T.H. Holland, Elizabeth's grandfather
Private Collection

My younger brother and I went to Canada in a convoy - that is to say a number of commandeered civilian vessels in the middle and naval vessels in a ring outside, all very low in the water with the sea breaking over them all the time. I thought nothing of it and it never occurred to me that we might drown. I was used to being surrounded by instruments of war - that was our life. We stayed in Canada with the family of my grandfather's sister, Elizabeth, in Winnipeg. **[fig.2]**. My grandfather, T.H. Holland, was a geologist, who worked for the Geological Survey in India before he took up appointments in Britain. He was a dedicated scientist and he - more than anyone else - was my ideal. **[fig.3]**. The notion of putting ideas in order is something I understand, but I have never felt a call to guerilla leadership or the blowing up of bridges.

On returning to England, I read History and Anthropology at Edinburgh University and later took an external degree with London University in Economics and International Relations. Before settling in Bath I had various occupations, which might be called community projects. At that time I was serious like my grandfather was in early life, and I felt that everything that one did should have social worth. I also did a great deal of writing. For a time I worked, chiefly as supply, in various homes for deprived children. I also spent a few years working in a residence in Edinburgh, founded by the former Rector of the University. There were many students from overseas there, especially doctors from India come to take higher degrees.

JPW: *What made you eventually set up home in Bath - and what career did you then follow?*

EAH: I did not in fact settle in Bath until the 1960s, although I had visited it previously when staying with my aunts, who lived in a beautiful William and Mary house in High Littleton. We had therefore gone into Bath on various occasions to eat sticky buns and visit the Roman Baths. **[fig. 4]**. My mother's grandfather was also Governor [i.e. Headmaster] at Kingswood School in his time. When the moment came to find a permanent place to live, I made a shortlist of possible cities and visited each in turn. However, as soon as I stepped off the train here, I knew that it would be Bath. I lectured part-time for some years in Economics and Social History, especially at what is now known as Bath College. I chose to teach older students at a college so that I could meet a wider range of people. These included many highly intelligent individuals from such places as Iraq and Persia - people who were actively involved in the politics of their own countries. This gave me, therefore, a window on the world.

JPW: *What first sparked your love of history?*

EAH: I had actually thought of reading English at university, but both my grandfathers persuaded me that history would provide a good education for both training the mind and fitting one for a useful career. I was not really interested in history *per se*, but in solving problems correctly. I like trying to grasp a given subject, whether it is history or not. For instance, with a friend and artist, Tim Brown, I have lately brought out a study called *The Pathway to the Tarot Trumps*. In this I searched for the meaning contained within the twenty-two pictures that are found in the pack of cards (dating back to around 1442) and came to the conclusion that these were illustrations of the 24th and 25th chapters of St. Matthew's gospel. But to answer your question, I suppose that my interest in studying the history of Bath was sparked by your own volume, *The Civil War in Bath and North Somerset* (1972), which showed me that one could discover facts about Bath instead of just the old legends.

JPW: *How did you come to establish The Survey of Old Bath?*

EAH: *The Civil War in Bath and North Somerset* led me to 'The Survey of Bath, 1641' in Bath Record Office, and I used it to plot all the property holders on John Speed's map of Bath dated 1610 (although it was apparently drawn in about 1575 by someone called Girtin). I became totally fascinated with this and realised that history could actually be interesting. In 1979, Tim O'Leary, working for Bath Archaeological Trust, suggested turning this into a scientific scale map using the resources of the Bath Record Office and other collections of documents. Tim and I chose the name 'Survey of Old Bath'. Mike Chapman, a surveyor and cartographer, joined the Survey in 1988, which was a major breakthrough. The Survey then began bringing out a number of publications - for we were now able to publish properly drawn maps. Since then we have received support and encouragement from a number of groups, including the Spa Project Team, Bath Archaeological Trust and Bath and North-East Somerset Council. In 1993, June Hodkinson founded the Friends of the Survey of Old Bath from a nucleus of supporters of the Stuart Age events, hosted by you at King Edward's School. They receive our journal, *The Survey of Old Bath and District*, which has recorded a great deal of new research.

JPW: *What has The Survey of Old Bath actually managed to achieve?*

EAH: The primary aim of the Survey as such was to locate specific sites within the old city (i.e. the old city as it existed before the nineteenth-century improvements). This has now been achieved - as, for example, with the 'Spa

Quarter' of the city, where every house has been identified century-by-century. You will also remember our discussion about the site of the original schoolhouse belonging to King Edward's at the time when you were writing the School's history. We have since extended our field to Widcombe and Lyncombe, and a number of old sites have been located there. I have worked closely on several projects with the Widcombe and Lyncombe History Study Group, of which I am a member.

The Survey has in fact been part of a general movement towards a more scientific assessment of Bath which took off during the eighties. This has been influenced by a number of factors besides the Survey - your own works, Bath Archaeological Trust, Trevor Fawcett's History of Bath Research Group, the new local societies, the publication of *Bath History*, Bath Record Office, the museums and so on. There has been a complete change of attitude towards our history, which is no longer based on guesswork.

JPW: *What are the main qualities you look for in a historian - and what annoys you most?*

EAH: The qualities one looks for - the absence of which is annoying - are the same as in any field, on a national as well as a local level: i.e. the willingness to take note of new research, instead of repeating old mistakes; acknowledging other people's work instead of writing as if it were one's own; and not bringing forward old ideas as if they were new ones. Particularly annoying in Bath, because of people's desire to make a name through the city's own reputation, is the habit of producing 'breakthroughs' - i.e. jumping to conclusions, refusing to discuss the evidence and publishing theories as if they were facts.

JPW: *How well does the city portray its history? What, if anything, is missing?*

EAH: The city is now quite well portrayed in print, because a mass of valuable work has been done of late. Nevertheless, in its portrayal to visitors, the Roman and Georgian periods still predominate - so there is no completely balanced view of its history. There are, however, three areas I most admire. Bath Record Office, which has been styled 'the Best in the West', is outstanding but needs more accommodation, funding and staff. A Local History Centre has been suggested, which would be valuable, provided it was directed by a well-qualified person like Colin Johnston, the Principal Archivist. I also admire the work of Stuart Burroughs at the Museum of Bath at Work, because it conveys something that was never previously presented - namely, the history of the city's ordinary people. Thirdly, I have been impressed with the Victoria Art Gallery, which has hosted a number of high-quality exhibitions.

JPW: *I know that you have produced a wonderful genealogy of the Chapman family - but why are you so interested in that family?*

EAH: My grandmother, Maud Holland, was a Chapman. Although she was born and married in India and her family before her, they always referred to themselves as the Chapmans of Bath. The Chapmans lived in the city for hundreds of years, which means that they interconnect with many of the old Bath families. They also owned a great deal of property locally - all of which ties in with the Survey of Old Bath. There were no fewer than eighteen known Chapman mayors of the city, who between them held the office thirty-five times. Furthermore, Peter Chapman, who was a distinguished soldier, made a

fig 5: Capt. Thomas Chapman
By courtesy of Herr Ludwig Becker, Herrnhut, Germany

major contribution to the restoration of Bath Abbey in the sixteenth century - the north aisle being named after him. I can tell you who each Chapman was, except for very minor figures. But there were also other distinguished Bath families, special in their own way (including the Atwoods). They deserve the same kind of publicity that the Chapmans have received.

JPW: *Of all the Chapmans you have researched, who is your favourite?*

EAH: It is without doubt Captain Thomas Chapman, who fought in the American War of Independence [1775-83]. A dashing young man, he fought with great valour and saved the life of his commanding officer. He was eventually taken prisoner, but - after being released on parole - eloped into the forest with the daughter of a Quaker settler. Her father insisted that they married. He later returned with his bride to England for a time, but subsequently died of yellow fever in San Domingo. **[fig. 5]**.

JPW: *Which of the seventeenth-century Chapmans is your favourite?*

EAH: Henry Chapman [1610-90], who was mayor in both 1664 and 1673 - because I enjoy his dashing, rounded character. But then you disapprove of him. [*An explanatory note from* **JPW**: Elizabeth is right - I do disapprove! He was guilty of political sleaze and electoral fraud long before the terms were invented. A royalist officer in the Civil War, he had been expelled from the local council for his delinquency. After the Restoration in 1660, he had become deeply frustrated that the old parliamentarian and puritan faction continued in power locally. He therefore attempted a political coup by kidnapping eleven of his opponents prior to the mayoral election of 1661 in a bid to win the vote. Although he was outmanoeuvred on this occasion, he did eventually become an impressive mayor, who helped to gain national fame for the health resort by launching an effective publicity campaign.]

JPW: *As an historian, do you approve of the recent development plans for the city?*

EAH: The Survey of Old Bath by its constitution has no opinions on planning matters. We supply information to both sides of a discussion, if they ask for it. When one sees the spirit of personal acrimony that seems to creep in, we are glad to remain outside!

JPW: *What ambitions do you still have in research and writing that are at present unfulfilled?*

EAH: My ambition is to make more of our work accessible to the public. The Survey would also appreciate funding for the maps still pending (similar to those of the Spa Quarter through the centuries) - i.e. the High Street and its area and the Walcot Street area. Material for these is already available, but the very detailed maps cannot be drawn for nothing. I also have an ambition to ensure that people always read what we have researched and written before they embark on the same subject. I read a long description of an old house the other day, except that the site being described did not relate to the house in question - as we could have told the writer instantly!

§

Footnote

Over the last twenty or so years, the Survey of Old Bath has been responsible for a wide range of publications, articles and exhibitions which cover neglected aspects of Bath's history. These have normally been produced jointly by Elizabeth Holland and Mike Chapman, although sometimes they have worked separately or occasionally in conjunction with other contributors (e.g. Peter Davenport, Giles White, John Hawkes and David McLaughlin). Several of the booklets have been funded by Avon County Council, Bath and North-East Somerset Council, the Millennium Commission or Bath Archaeological Trust.

The booklets include *Citizens of Bath* (1989); *The Story of the White Hart* (1990); *The Kingston Estate within the Walled City: a Composite Plan of the 1740s* (1992); *Bath and the Warwick Book of Hours* (1994); *A Guide to the Estates of Ralph Allen around Bath* (1996); *The J. Charlton Map of Lyncombe and Widcombe, 1799* (1997); *An Historical Analysis of the Corridor Area* (1999); *Baths and Pump Rooms of Bath; an Historical Summary* (2000); *'Bimbery' and the South-Western Baths of Bath* (2001); *The Lost Streams of Bath* (2003); and *The Spa Quarter of Bath, a History in Maps* (2006). A forthcoming publication in 2008 is volume one of a projected new series, 'Records of Bath': *Papers of the Ralph Allen Estate and Other Documents*.

Articles include two which have appeared in *Bath History* - 'The Earliest Bath Guildhall', volume II (1988); and 'The Development of Saw Close from the Middle Ages', volume VIII (2000). There have been numerous articles in *The Survey of Bath and District: The Journal of the Survey of Old Bath*, including a series entitled 'This Famous City: the Story of the Chapmans of Bath'. 'The Precincts of the Bishops' Palace at Bath, Avon' was published in *The Archaeological Journal*, volume 152 (1995) and 'Stothert's Foundry, Southgate Street, Bath' in the *BIAS Journal*, number 30 (1998).

Two exhibitions produced by the Survey are also worth recording - *The Baths of Bath* exhibition (1988) and *The Holloway Street at Bath and its Neighbourhood* exhibition at the Museum of Bath at Work, which is planned for April 2009 in collaboration with the Widcombe and Lyncombe History Study Group. There is in addition an illuminated genealogy *The Descent of the Chapman Mayors of Bath in the Seventeenth Century*, which was presented to Bath Record Office in 1989 (Accession 170). The display boards of *The Baths of Baths* exhibition are also located there.

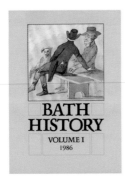

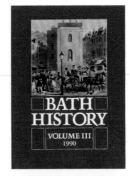

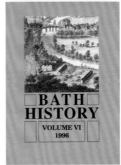

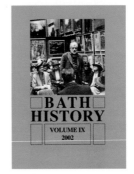

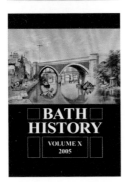

A full index of all previously published articles is available in Bath History Vol. X.